CURTAIN WALLS

Cesar Pelli

MICHAEL J. CROSBIE

CURTAIN WALLS

RECENT DEVELOPMENTS
BY CESAR PELLI & ASSOCIATES

BIRKHÄUSER – PUBLISHERS FOR ARCHITECTURE
BASEL · BERLIN · BOSTON

We would like to express our appreciation to the architects and designers of Cesar Pelli & Associates and to our consultants whose creative work appears in this book. The making of this book has been a collaborative process with contributions from many. Mike Crosbie coherently and clearly describes a highly technical subject matter. Mig Halpine and Ben Charney coordinated project documentation, photography, and illustrations. Pablo Lopez produced many of the architectural drawings. Special thanks to Ria Stein for her guidance and attention to detail throughout the design and production of this book. We would also like to recognize Esther Mildenberger and Brian Switzer of envision+ for the design and layout of the book.

Cesar Pelli, Fred Clarke and Rafael Pelli

Design: envision+
www.envisionplus.com

A CIP catalogue record for this book is available from the Library of Congress, Washington D.C., USA

Bibliographic information published by Die Deutsche Bibliothek
Die Deutsche Bibliothek lists this publication in the Deutsche Nationalbibliografie; detailed bibliographic data is available in the internet at http://dnb.ddb.de.

2005 Birkhäuser – Publishers for Architecture, P.O. Box 133, CH-4010 Basel, Switzerland
Part of Springer Science+Business Media
Printed on acid-free paper produced from chlorine-free pulp. TCF ∞
Printed in Germany
ISBN-13: 978-3-7643-7083-1
ISBN-10: 3-7643-7083-1

www.birkhauser.ch

9 8 7 6 5 4 3 2 1

CONTENTS

THE ART AND CRAFT OF
CESAR PELLI'S CURTAIN WALLS

Crystal Palace, Joseph Paxton, London, 1851

In the architecture of Cesar Pelli, there is no part of the building that has been the subject of more critical attention than simply "the wall." The veil that separates interior from exterior, demarcating where the building begins, is for Pelli and his collaborators its most expressive element – an epidermis through which architectural ideas are communicated. Indeed, Pelli's very surname, in Spanish, means "skins."

Over Pelli's 50-year career, during which he has practiced with Eero Saarinen, Victor Gruen, and the firm Daniel Mann Johnson and Mendenhall (in addition to heading his own practice for the past 28 years), Pelli's designs for exterior curtain walls weave like filaments that glow with the heat of intellectual curiosity and the light of architectural experimentation.

Recognizing the major shift in building construction that started with Joseph Paxton's Crystal Palace of 1851 (of which Pelli has written extensively) and accelerated after World War II (when enclosing walls became more independent of the structure) Pelli has focused on expressing this new reality. He brilliantly conceived of a new architectonic paradigm for the modern building: the traditional tropical hut made of a lightweight frame of cane and covered with a thin skin of grass. His curtain wall explorations are guided by this belief: that architecture as an art and a craft can advance only when new ideas are tested against the possibilities of contemporary construction.

Nature of the Curtain Wall

Born in the firmament of the Industrial Revolution, and the offspring of Paxton's shimmering glass sheath, the curtain wall is one of the best examples of modern architecture's quest for the incredible lightness of buildings. Over architecture's long history, buildings have become progressively less earth-bound, their enclosures more shear and ethereal. The development of the curtain wall in the late 1800s separated the building's enclosure from its structure, making the two essentially

independent. In a curtain wall the exterior enclosure hangs, akin to a curtain, from a structural frame of steel or concrete (the Statue of Liberty, constructed in 1884 with an iron frame supporting a light-weight cladding of thin copper, is one of the earliest examples of a curtain wall in the U.S.).

After World War II, technical advances in the performance of glazing, sheet metal, and gaskets allowed the walls to become thinner and more energy-efficient. Today curtain walls are prefabricated, consisting of panels mounted into a metal frame attached to the building's structure. Opaque curtain wall "spandrel panels" can be finished in virtually any material, but metal and stone are the most common. The "vision panels" are made of insulated, multi-pane glass, with a variety of coatings for appearance and performance.

Older style "stick systems," where the curtain wall is composed of individual elements (glass, mullions, gaskets, spandrel panels, metal caps) assembled on-site, have given way to prefabricated "unitized systems" that arrive at the construction site virtually preassembled, ready to be lifted into place and fastened to the building's structure. While unitized systems now dominate curtain wall technology, stick style systems continue to be used in some parts of the world.

Most curtain wall buildings are made with "off-the-shelf" systems designed by curtain wall manufacturers, and they are pretty prosaic and uninspired. The design challenge for architects such as Cesar Pelli & Associates is to take the elements of contemporary curtain wall systems and interpret them in new ways, expressing the architectonic character of the wall as central to the building's architectural presence. Pelli achieves this through custom-designed and fabricated curtain walls that are special to the place, function, and architectural aspirations of the building.

Seagram Building, Ludwig Mies van der Rohe, New York, 1958

Carson, Pirie, Scott and Company Building, Louis Sullivan, Chicago, 1899

Hallidie Building, Willis Polk, San Francisco, 1918

Curtain Walls of Invention

Cesar Pelli and his curtain wall design collaborators – Fred Clarke (a firm principal who helped Pelli found the practice in 1977), Gregg Jones, Lawrence Ng, and (more recently) Rafael Pelli – tint their architectonic investigations of the wall with the realities of every project they work on. Of all the elements that appear to influence Pelli's design of a curtain wall, the most important is context. While contextual response in the design of tall buildings was evident in the work of the early skyscraper architects (such as Louis Sullivan) by the post-war period it became all but lost. Architects vacillated between two extremes: the more talented (such as Mies van der Rohe) applied what they considered "universal" design solutions to every design problem they faced, replicating them without concern for local architectural character. Mies' less-talented followers populated the skylines with cheap knock-offs that were alien behemoths. Every place became nowhere in particular.

Pelli revived the tradition of the contextually responsive tall building, and it has become stronger in the firm's work over the years. Cesar Pelli & Associates marries the tall building to its place in the city, creating a unity between the two. As Pelli himself expresses it: "The curtain wall, like the rest of the building's design, needs to adjust itself to the unique conditions of each place, the urban responsibility of the building, and the uniqueness of its functions."

The building's form, materials, and details all work to reinforce the connection of the building with its role in the city. For Pelli the first responsibility of any building is to support the civic life of the city and its cultural identity. All of Pelli's curtain wall designs flow from this system of values and priorities.

According to CP&A's Lawrence Ng, the Pelli team believes that the job of the architect is "to give the client's aspirations for the project artistic rendition." Often clients cannot verbalize what their architectural aspirations are and they describe them in non-architectural terms: They want their building to be "solid," or "lasting," or a "beacon." These visions then direct Pelli's search for an expression – how the curtain wall can help achieve these formal goals. Ideas are cultivated, multiple options are developed for clients to respond to, and a design emerges from this give and take. Says Ng: "Architecture is a collaborative art. For us, it is very much an interactive process with the client."

The Function of Form

What drives the design of a curtain wall? According to Pelli and Clarke, the building's form is the genesis of the architecture. Generally, curtain walls are designed to serve the building's architectural form, particularly towers that will take a prominent place on the skyline. Every decision about the curtain wall's design is driven by its service to the large ideas concerning architectural form and its expression. "The form is the greatest expression of a tall building," says Pelli. "That is the first level, and the design of the curtain wall supports that role. That is the hierarchy."

Pelli often chooses to clad his buildings in materials that forge connections with the local context or recall the indigenous culture, such as native Kasota stone for a curtain wall in Minnesota, or ceramic tile for a Japanese high rise. Pelli believes that the design of the curtain wall must be respectful of the regional character, reflecting its symbolism and local color. This was literally true in the case of the JP Morgan Chase high rise in San Francisco, completed in 2002, whose green color is an homage to the city's first modern curtain wall structure, the Hallidie Building, built in 1918.

Another way to describe Pelli's architecture is as either "form active" or "form passive." Form active buildings, primarily towers, convey a strong formal presence on the skyline – they

Pacific Design Center, West Hollywood, 1971   Detail of San Bernardino City Hall, 1972

are sculptural objects whose overall form is clearly expressed, especially from a distance. Form passive buildings are less overt in their formal expression, and tend to be low-rise structures. In either case, the approach to the curtain wall design takes a different tact. Form active buildings generally have curtain walls of less depth and tauter surfaces (allowing the overall form of the building to be read most clearly), while form passive designs use curtain walls that are more three-dimensional and woven with depth.

If the form is to read as a single silhouette on the skyline, then a sleek and highly reflective surface often serves as the strongest expression of that form. If, however, the building is more modest in its scale, and less of an object on the skyline, then the curtain wall design will be more three-dimensional and deep, which can be appreciated from the vantage point of the sidewalk, or from across the street, or just down the block.

However, this is not always the case. Pelli has used taut, sleek skins on low-rise buildings, such as the San Bernardino City Hall (completed in 1972) and the Pacific Design Center (1975). Conversely, deep, three-dimensional curtain walls can be found in some of Pelli's tallest buildings, such as the Petronas Towers (1997). The City Hall and the Design Center are perhaps the most radically sleek curtain walls of minimal depth that Pelli has ever produced. In these projects, the wall expresses the building as an extrusion or a sculptural object. At San Bernardino, Pelli pushed the limits of cladding a building completely in glass (used for both the vision and spandrel panels) with slender aluminum mullions. The Design Center's bright blue curtain wall wraps every element of the building-roof, wall, soffit, and vault – with little or no expression of what is behind the sleek, reflective surface. A later addition by Pelli to the Design Center of a separate building in green took a similar approach, using the curtain wall as veritable wrapping paper.

At the Petronas Tower, the curtain wall works to express the form, yet it has an identity all its own. From afar, the form of the building is forcefully expressed in the slender, stepped, contextual silhouettes of the towers. Closer views of the buildings bring a new reading and appreciation of complexity through the deep horizontal shading devices over the windows, which serve as a counterpoint to the towers' overall vertical expression. Pelli has used such shading devices in other buildings, such as the NTT Headquarters (1995), 1500 Louisiana (2001), and others, which give them much texture and depth. From inside the building they provide a sense of enclosure – a ledge that surrounds the tower and gives the occupants the psychological equivalent of a safety belt.

Over the past decade-and-a-half, Pelli's curtain walls have become more three-dimensional and richer in their depth. The Petronas Towers are a good example of this direction, reveling in their depth and shadow. In Malaysia, near the equator, the air is infused with sunlight. Petronas expresses this environmental condition in its deep sunshades, which completely encircle each tower. In Hong Kong, the Cheung Kong Center (1999) literally sparkles, its ebullient surface bristling with projected floodlights that provide another textured layer and transform the tower into a lantern whose linen-finished stainless steel mullions appear to magically glow from within.

The evolution of Pelli's curtain wall designs is also evident in the different kinds of materials and detailing that he is using today that were not part of his architectural vocabulary 10 or 15 years ago. This is due primarily to the fact the firm's work now extends around the world. As each new context demands a response specific to it, Pelli's vocabulary of materials and detailing becomes richer. There is a greater variety of materials used, the detailing is more sophisticated, and the curtain walls have become deeper and more complex.

World Financial Center, New York

Cheung Kong Center, Hong Kong

Scale and Expression

Scale is an important design issue to Pelli. He derives different readings of the building depending on the context. The building's variety of scales is expressed in the curtain wall's design. Tall buildings are perceived most elementally as two images: one on the skyline and the other on the sidewalk. For example, when one stands at the base of the Chrysler Building in New York City you are barely aware of the building's exuberant stainless steel crown. Viewing the building from close proximity, one can appreciate the rich Art Deco ornament at the base – the materials, details, proportions, and pedestrian scale. From this perspective (and depending on the width of the street and the open space around the building) only the first 10 meters of the tower can be seen. The design of this portion of the building places greater emphasis on detailing appreciated from close range. Above this height the curtain wall transitions from one read from nearby on the ground, to one appreciated from the sky, moving from the eye of man to the eye of God, much the way cathedrals were designed hundreds of years ago.

The unity of the tall building's form is tempered with the expression of its interior arrangement of layers of floors. A sleek glass surface that obscures the expression of floors, such as the Cira Centre (2005) in Philadelphia, reveals the layered arrangement primarily at night, when the floors are easily perceived.

In some of Pelli's towers the reading of the curtain wall as either horizontal or vertical is ambiguous, such as in the 777 Tower (1990) in Los Angeles, where the building's form transcends the directional nature of the curtain wall. This is also the case with an earlier project, the World Financial Center (1988) in Battery Park City, New York, where the curtain wall does not express a horizontal or vertical direction, yet its windows grow in size and expression as successive layers of the towers peel back. This curtain wall transforms from one that feels nearly balanced in the mix of solid and glass at the base, to one that blooms with larger pieces of glass in the upper stories. Yet the directional expression of the curtain wall remains neutral throughout – neither horizontal nor vertical – while the skin is taut on all four sides.

Occasionally Pelli mixes horizontal and vertical curtain wall expressions to denote different building uses. In the two towers of the Atago Green Hills (2001) development in Tokyo, the curtain wall of the Mori Office Tower reads as a vertical skin, while the Forest Residential Tower curtain wall's expression is horizontal. This is entirely consistent for the functions found within. The vertical expression is best suited to repetitive commercial office space that tends to be experienced as taller than it is wide. In the sky, the form of a human being in front of the vertical window gives these buildings a scale perceptible from the ground and from other tall buildings. In apartment buildings there is more of a horizontal unity of spaces, which on the curtain wall can be read as individual living units made up of several spaces that stretch across the façade (especially at night, when they are illuminated).

Illumination is a key ingredient in reading the Cheung Kong Center. During the day, the predominant perception is of a vertical building, as the perpendicular stainless steel mullions catch the sun and emphasize this dimension. At night, the building blazes with lights both inside and out, which make it glow like a beacon. Under these conditions, the tower reads more as a composition of horizontal layers, which reinforces its appearance as a lantern.

The Curtain Wall Process

The curtain wall is one of the more costly elements of a building, the others being structure, mechanical systems, and elevators. The design phase of a commercial tower can be very short – sometimes the building can start fast-track

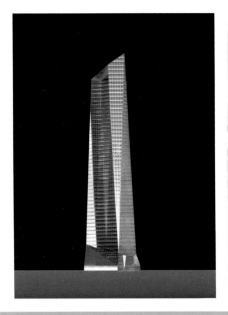

Torre de Cristal study model   **Torre Libertad rendering**

construction in as little as six months after going under contract. In the creation of custom-designed curtain walls, decisions must be made with just the right balance of careful consideration and speed. The key is to "manage the risk of making those decisions early," as Fred Clarke explains it. Once critical selections of the curtain wall's design elements are finalized – particularly materials, finishes, and arrangement – changing one's mind can be very costly.

"Among the team members, we are the ones protecting the esthetic values of the curtain wall," notes Clarke, because the client does not want to pay any more for this element of the building than is budgeted for it. The depth and range of the design team's experience is critical here, because the design of the curtain wall is full of interlocking decisions. For example, how might the choice of either stainless steel or aluminum affect the cost of attaining a consistent finish that supports the esthetic goals of the design, or what is the availability of the material to avoid a time lag in fabrication, which would slow the construction down on other fronts?

According to curtain wall consultant Bill Logan of Israel Berger Associates, who has a long history of collaboration with CP&A, one of the keys to Pelli's success is the wealth of curtain wall knowledge that the firm possesses. "Pelli's office has a 'deep team,'" says Logan, referring to the number of associates and principals who know curtain wall systems intimately. "Because of his extensive work, Cesar has built a core group of experienced architects. Each associate takes on many responsibilities. Cesar has direct oversight, but he delegates a lot of responsibility."

Working with curtain wall consultants and having collaborative relationships with a variety of fabricators allows CP&A to manage the risk of early decision-making. CP&A works with curtain wall consultants on projects around the globe, although the number of these professionals consulted on a regular basis

is small – Larry Ng estimates that there are no more than a half-dozen people worldwide that can deliver the services that the firm demands. CP&A has found that it is best to bring the curtain wall consultant in on a project as early as possible, once the formal goals of the building have been articulated. At this point, the curtain wall consultant works with CP&A to determine the most efficient way to satisfy the design goals of the building through its enclosure: the choice of materials and their dimensions, color, finish, and arrangement, and the cost implications. Occasionally, several materials (each of which would fulfill the esthetic goals of the building) will be considered for a single curtain wall. One Canada Square (1991) at Canary Wharf in London, for instance, was designed as both a stainless steel and a stone-clad curtain wall – with working drawings prepared for both materials (it was ultimately constructed in stainless steel).

Curtain Wall Consultants

The consultant often is helpful in selecting a curtain wall manufacturer, based on his or her knowledge of the company's track-record and its ability to accomplish the work sought. In some cases two manufacturers are selected to create a competitive environment (this was the case for the Petronas Towers, each of which had a different curtain wall manufacturer).

For projects in North America and Asia, curtain wall consultants usually become involved in the project just after schematic design, once the project has been defined in its broad strokes. According to Bill Logan, "The Pelli team at this point has a vision of the form and the scale of the building. We attempt to understand their goals and come up with different approaches – Cesar likes to see a range of options and study which fits best with the formal concept."

For example, if the goal of a tower design is to express transparency, CP&A and the curtain wall consultant might

Detail of Mori Tower canopy

consider all the ways that this could be accomplished, developing perhaps a half-dozen basic concepts that often start with a structural approach: how the curtain wall is to be supported. The different approaches are then exhaustively studied in model form – both computer and physical models at a range of scales, becoming more and more detailed as the design is refined. Pelli works extensively with three-dimensional models – a method of design exploration that he cultivated during his years with Saarinen.

Quick study models for massing and scale give way to more detailed ones where pieces are quickly changed, removed, and new elements pasted on as the architects study alternatives. The refining process moves up in scale, the overall formal ideas are set, and details are worked out to support the larger design goals. Clients know that the four or five options presented by CP&A are the result of intensive studies. For example, on 560 Mission Street in San Francisco, the Pelli team showed the client the more than 40 variations of the color green considered for the exterior to demonstrate the architect's exhaustive search for just the right shade.

Gradually this procedure culminates in full-scale mock-ups, which are built by the fabricator/manufacturer. Throughout the process the curtain wall consultant continues to serve as a sounding board for the Pelli team's ideas, offering insight into cost implications, the limits and requirements of materials and fabrication techniques, alternative support options, specifications, shop-drawing reviews – all in support of CP&A's esthetic goals for the project.

Since he or she is working directly with the curtain wall fabricator or manufacturer, the curtain wall consultant can serve as a powerful advocate for Pelli's vision. "We can nudge these people, in a sympathetic way, to do their best work because we understand the concerns of both parties," Logan explains, in looking at alternatives and exhausting all of the

possibilities to meet the design goals for the curtain wall. Generally, curtain wall manufacturers and fabricators covet Pelli jobs because they are high-profile buildings that will be recognized around the world. "They are eager to work with Cesar, knowing that the building will showcase their abilities and products," explains Logan. They are usually willing to meet more often to develop creative engineering approaches.

For projects in Europe, curtain wall consultants play less of a role because the Pelli team starts working from day one with curtain wall manufacturers and suppliers to understand the predominant systems used locally, the technical possibilities and cost impacts, and the skill level of contractors. Today in Europe, curtain walls are more technologically advanced than they are in North America (energy performance is much more stringent), so engineering expertise (thermal performance, especially) is highly critical on these projects.

The Pelli team stresses working first-hand with local or regional curtain wall manufacturers and contractors in certain parts of the world, such as South America, where use of international systems is not likely. "With a new project, you speak immediately with local manufacturers, with whom you work in parallel," says Edward Dionne, who is CP&A's project manager for the Torre Libertad (2006) in Mexico City. "They provide a reality check all the way along, and you know that all the options have been considered. We thus know that the contractors are familiar with the curtain wall systems chosen."

In these cases, the local skill level must be able to support the use of the curtain wall selected. For example, if stick systems rather than unitized systems are predominant in this part of the world, then CP&A works within that context. In another instance, curtain wall anchoring systems are not standardized. Different anchoring techniques require different structural tolerances (some are more forgiving than others). Knowing the local skill level and construction tolerances for

Sculptural form under construction,
National Museum of Art, Osaka

Curtain wall performance mock-up,
International Finance Centre

structural frames in Hong Kong had a direct affect on the detailing of the curtain wall anchor for the International Finance Centre (2004). Working with local experts is key to understanding the scores of local conventions that will affect construction.

Curtain Wall Mock-Ups

As the curtain wall design moves into its final stages, full-scale mock-ups of the wall are made to study its appearance and performance. Even though computer models have become more realistic, they go only so far in rendering the curtain wall as it will actually be experienced. Computer renderings cannot convey how reflections will appear. Materials such as granite, slate, and stainless steel are very subtle in their texture, color, grain, reflectivity, fabrication marks, and minute imperfections. For example, differences in pressure in a rolling press that produces stainless steel curtain wall panels can affect how the material will look after it is installed.

Two types of mock-ups are used: "visual" and "performance." Larry Ng refers to visual mock-ups as "three-dimensional design drawings" that show the location and size of the joints, the interface of various curtain wall elements, and (most importantly) the appearance of the glass. All the parties involved – the client, architect, contractor, various consultants, and the fabricator – study the visual mock-up to evaluate a plethora of issues. For example, how materials and their finishes will appear under different weather and lighting conditions (including artificial light); how shadow lines will be read; the visual impact of the width of the mullions; the color and transparency of the glass; how the glass appearance contributes to reading the building's scale; and the reflectivity and opacity of glass frit patterns. A visual mock-up can be constructed at the fabricator's plant or on the building site. The mock-up can be raised and lowered to study it from different vantage points, including from the inside looking out. This is the last chance to make

adjustments in the curtain wall's design. Once fabrication begins, changes can be very costly.

Every curtain wall designed by CP&A undergoes testing via performance or technical mock-ups to study air and water infiltration, condensation, and how the curtain wall reacts to temperature extremes and movement. At testing labs in Florida, Pennsylvania, and California, or at contractors' facilities around the globe, full-scale curtain wall performance mock-ups for buildings all over the world are constructed and then subjected to such tests as water propelled by aircraft engines, simulating hurricane-force gales. The mock-ups undergo days of such testing, allowing CP&A and its team of consultants to confirm structural behavior and to make adjustments to the design to thwart any water or air leakage before the curtain wall goes into production.

Time and Money

What is CP&A's time-frame for creating a curtain wall? For a 200-meter-tall building, the entire process will typically take approximately 30 months from the award of the curtain wall contract to the complete installation of the system. From the start to the first installation of a panel, about 10 to 12 months is to be expected. The first six months of the process are very intense, with the development of three-dimensional proposal drawings, visual mock-ups, technical testing, and the preparation of shop drawings. Glass and all of the other materials for the cladding are ordered. When construction commences, the Pelli team is attentive as to whether installation tolerances are being met. The first few panels are the key ones. Once a control reference of tolerances is established, the curtain wall installation is fairly straight-forward.

Part of CP&A's expertise is a detailed understanding of how the curtain wall industry operates and how costs are affected. Curtain wall costs are driven by many factors, but the three

Detail view of COMSAT Laboratories

biggest are: the amount of extruded material used; the choice of glass; and the installation procedure. Any one of these factors is a potentially volatile ingredient in the curtain wall budget. For example, in Europe between 2001 and 2003, the cost of glass shot up by 60 percent. As construction activity has slowed, the cost has since come down. Installation costs are much higher in the U.S. than in Europe due the influence of labor unions. The industry is constantly consolidating, and the universe of curtain wall manufacturers is shrinking. In North America, there are only four companies (Benson, Enclos [Cupples], Antamex, and Permasteelisa) that can produce large-scale curtain wall jobs. In Europe there are only two major companies: Permasteelisa and Schwalin, with a scattering of smaller operations serving the curtain wall niche market. Most of the large manufacturers will not bother with small jobs. Such factors are all part of the mix in designing a curtain wall.

Material Evolution

Over the past 35 years, since some of Pelli's earliest curtain wall buildings such as the COMSAT Laboratories (1969) in Clarksburg, Maryland, curtain wall technology has grown by leaps and bounds. As mentioned before, curtain wall systems now use more prefabricated elements, delivered to the site in a unitized fashion that allows whole sections of the wall to be raised and secured in place. In the aftermath of some curtain wall system failures in the 1980s, more attention is now given to material sizes, durability, and anchoring techniques (usually steel anchors welded to the backside of curtain wall panels, which are then hung on the curtain wall frame and tied back into the building's structure). Computer analysis now allows curtain wall fabricators to model how systems might perform in high winds and during earthquakes. This computer modeling is backed up with on-site testing of various curtain wall mock-ups.

The range of materials used in curtain walls has expanded. Granite and aluminum – the old standby materials – are now joined by such novel cladding as slate, tile, limestone, sandstone, titanium, stainless steel (Pelli virtually resuscitated its use in architecture), and a wealth of sophisticated coatings for metal. Stone for curtain walls is being sliced thinner and is more exact in its thickness and tolerance.

Energy Performance

The greatest recent technical curtain wall breakthroughs have been in glass technology. There are now larger pieces of glass in more complex shapes, curved glass, better insulating glazing units, advanced coatings to mitigate heat gain and loss, a wide range of reflective coatings, clearer glass formulations, and laminations resulting in shatter-resistant glazings for better security. Glass frits expand the variety.

One of the major drivers in CP&A's curtain wall design work around the world is energy performance. While in Europe and Asia this has long been in the case, even in the U.S. more high-rise buildings are being designed for LEED certification (the U.S. Green Building Council's Leadership in Energy and Environmental Design rating system, which recognizes different levels of energy conservation and sustainability). CP&A is finding ways to make curtain walls more energy-efficient, such as increased insulation levels and the use of shading devices that cut heat gain while bouncing reflected light deeper into the building. The external sunshades on the Petronas Towers are a good example: they help ease the energy needs of the building and are part of the architectural vocabulary of the tropics.

The major arena of innovation is in high-performance glazing that can help reduce cooling loads in hot weather and mitigate heat loss in cold weather. The current thrust in CP&A's curtain wall design is to achieve greater transparency (glass that is clearer, with little or no tinting) while maintaining

Detail of Petronas Towers curtain wall

energy conservation. Low-emissivity glass coatings (low-e) reduce the U-value of glass and boost its thermal performance, while better shading coefficients help block radiant heat from passing through the glass in the summer. Pelli is using more low-iron-content glass, which has greater transparency and almost no perceptible tinting. Less obstructed views into the building enhance its human scale (occupants can easily be seen), while clearer views out render the environment in its true color and light. Many of Pelli's curtain wall designs are a delicate balance of transparency and reflectivity. The glass in the 30 Hudson Street tower, for example, has just enough reflectivity so that it is perceived as a solid object on the skyline. Closer up, views of office workers contribute to the building's human scale.

High-performance glazing means that larger areas of vision glass are possible without compromising energy conservation. Pelli's work reflects this: his curtain walls are more transparent than they were 20 years ago. Dark-tinted windows have fallen out of favor. Today office workers expect to have a stronger visual relationship with the world beyond their cubicles, and clients are asking for clearer, low-iron-content glass that renders the environment in its natural colors, maximizing views and bringing more light into the building. The balance is between good energy efficiency and perfectly clear glass.

Glass Frits

Pelli's curtain walls for years have made inventive use of frit patterns on glass-enamel paint on the glazing surface that can help reduce glare, contribute to the building's scale and identity, enhance privacy, and allow the glass surface to be easily seen when illuminated at night. Frits are silk-screened onto the glass, usually on the number 2 or 3 surface of double-glazed units. Clients for commercial buildings, particularly offices with multiple tenants, typically do not want the

type of strong, non-uniform visual identities that fritted glass can provide. For institutional buildings, Pelli has effectively used frits to supplement the building's design narrative. In the Minneapolis Central Library (2006), for instance, the glass frit design becomes an allegory of the building's place in the Minnesota landscape. The library's four exterior walls have frit designs that each tells a different story. On the side that faces Nicollet Street, the frit appears as white birch trees that allude to the forest. On the side facing the Mississippi River, the frit replicates ripples of water. On the north side the frit design depicts prairie grasses, while to the south the frit patterns appear as snow.

Curtain Wall Lighting

The next major technical advance is in curtain wall illumination, and CP&A has already incorporated artificial light as a design element. The firm's curtain wall designs have included sophisticated lighting schemes, depending on the wishes of the client.

At 280 meters tall, it would have been impossible to floodlight the entire Cheung Kong Center building façade in Hong Kong, which is stainless steel. This material does not reflect light evenly as a stone surface might, so the light sources themselves have to be evenly distributed.

Light is nearly an indigenous material for tall buildings in Hong Kong and has become a cultural phenomenon – millions are spent in turning skyscrapers into lavish light shows. CP&A incorporated fiber-optic lighting into the curtain wall mullions (at the intersection of horizontal and vertical members) along with floodlights mounted on short outriggers that cover the tower's exterior. The floods make the building glow, as the light is reflected in the stainless steel's linen finish, illuminating it like a lantern. The fiber-optic lights are programmed by computer and can animate the building's surface, transforming it into a canvas of color and movement. At the Cira Centre in

Detail of Cheung Kong Center curtain wall

Philadelphia, clusters of light-emitting diodes (LEDs) are incorporated directly into the curtain wall's spandrel panels in a 5-meter grid.

A Note on Project Organization

The following sections of this book, which present CP&A's most advanced curtain wall projects, are organized according to the predominant materials used in each wall: glass, stone, or metal. Such an organization allows each of these materials to be compared and contrasted. In many cases, a material is chosen by CP&A to achieve a certain esthetic goal or architectural expression. Studying how the same material is implemented across a number of projects reveals the inventiveness of the designers, and demonstrates how certain materials have evolved in their use by Pelli over time (especially glass and metal).

Grouping the curtain walls by material also allows close comparisons between buildings of the same material as the work spans across the years. For example, Pelli's curtain walls generally have become more three-dimensional in their composition. Comparing Pelli's later curtain walls in glass to metal curtain walls of the same period reveals how the design thread of three-dimensional form- making is accomplished in different materials. Such comparisons can be made not only on the outward appearance of the curtain wall, but also in its inner details, which are rendered through the exacting drawings and details that document the curtain wall designs in the following sections.

In addition to the photographs and drawings, each project profile documents the context and site conditions, the design ideas that are the basis for architectural form and its expression, and the components of the finished curtain wall that support the larger design goals of the project.

If you study these curtain wall projects as embodiments of Pelli's own values as an architect, it is likely that you will discover architecture that is mindful of its place, its time, and the way in which it is constructed. As such, these buildings tell us as much about the architects who created them.

GLASS

TORRE BANKBOSTON
BUENOS AIRES

A
East elevation, scale 1:750

B
Site plan

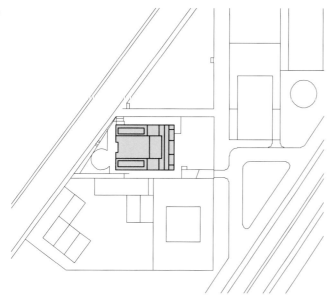

Context and Site: The BankBoston headquarters building site is located in the Catalinas Norte district in downtown Buenos Aires. Two main avenues border this area: Avenida Madero to the north, facing the river, and Avenida Alem to the south, which defines the beginning of the traditional urban fabric. Catalinas Norte is a special district with its own design guidelines. The guidelines, written in the 1960s, reflect the esthetic preferences of the time. They have spawned buildings shaped as prismatic towers with simple lines, clearly delineated edges – and flat tops. Although Torre BankBoston has tall buildings nearby, the density of the site is such that the building is read as its own figural element against the sky, with water on one side and the city on the other.

Architectural Form and Expression: The 45,000-square-meter BankBoston headquarters follows the district's design guidelines but reinterprets them in a contemporary spirit. The 137-meter tower starts from the base as a very simple volume that blossoms with sculptural forms as it reaches the sky. A series of setbacks with increasingly slanted walls create a distinct profile, while near the top a counter-sloped cap emerges like a reed to terminate the building. Torre BankBoston is not a mute prism, but a place marker enriching the character of the city silhouette.

Curtain Wall Components: The curtain wall is designed as a taut and lively skin, supporting the overall esthetic goals of the building as an active sculptural object. At the bottom of the tower, the 10-meter-high base steps out to welcome visitors, and the curtain wall is rendered in stainless steel.

Above the base, a complex two-directional pattern is described by a series of half-round horizontal and vertical mullions. The clear anodized aluminum tartan grid of the mullions catches the light either vertically or horizontally; depending on the time of day, the building changes its directional emphasis. Double column covers in aluminum race up and down the façade (and also conceal window-washing tracks). The tower's central crown employs dark anodized aluminum mullions and accents (as it faces the water, the crown conceals a mechanical penthouse).

Varieties of glass give expression to the tower's different elements. The body of the building is rendered in a Viracon insulated glass with a reflective coating. This material is used for the spandrel panels (although not insulated) as well as for the vision glass. The glass reflectivity and the shallow depth of the mullions both work to give prominence to the reading of the overall building form. A tinted vision panel is used in the central portion of the tower top. In the mechanical penthouse (which contains telecommunications equipment) the dark green opaque glass is transparent to the transmission of microwave signals and contrasts with the body of the tower, providing the headquarters with an appropriately ceremonial terminus against the sky. At the base, clear glass is used to emphasize the lobby and to communicate a sense of welcoming transparency.

C

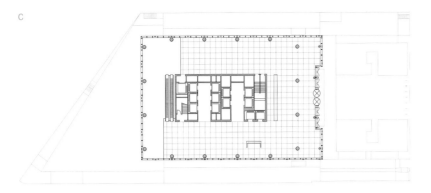

D

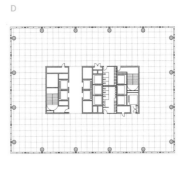

Tower top looking towards Río De La Plata

Setbacks looking towards the city

South-west corner curtain wall detail

E

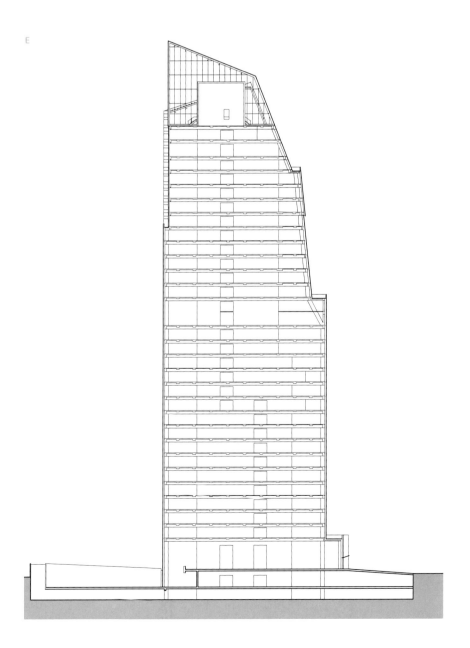

Tower top curtain wall installation

Building under construction from Avenida Alem

Tower top under construction

View from Avenida Alem

F
Section detail through north elevation
second setback
1 Roof construction: precast concrete pavers,
  thermal insulation, waterproof layer
2 Aluminum sheet bent to shape
3 Monolithic spandrel glass with 6mm clear
  heat-strengthened glass, ceramic frit on #2
  surface, custom color polyester opacifier
4 Tinted low-e insulated glass: 6mm blue/green
  heat-strengthened glass,
  low-e coating on #2 surface, 13mm airspace,
  6mm clear glass
5 Dark bronze anodized aluminum mullion
6 Insulation
7 Internal glare protection
8 Gypsum plaster board
9 Clear anodized aluminum mullion

G
Section detail through south elevation setback
10 Reflective monolithic spandrel glass: 6mm
   clear heat-strengthened glass, low-e coating
   on #2 surface, polyester opacifier
11 Reflective insulating glass: 6mm clear heat-
   strengthened glass, low-e coating on #2
   surface, 13mm airspace, 6mm clear glass

Location
Buenos Aires, Argentina
Dates
1997–2000
Client
US Equities, BankBoston-Argentina
Building Program
Headquarters
Height
137 meters; 35 floors
Building Structural System
Reinforced concrete
Curtain Wall Type
Unitized
Mullions
Anodized aluminum
Spandrel Panels
Spandrel glass
Glass Type
Vision: reflective glass
Spandrel: reflective glass with
polyester opacifier
Storefront vision: clear glass with

low-e coating Storefront accent bands: clear
glass with low-e coating and ceramic frit pattern
Top vision: tinted glass with low-e coating
Top spandrel: ceramic frit
Lighting
Uplights at ground floor level grazing the
elevation of the tower
Curtain Wall Manufacturer
Exxal
CP&A Project Team
Design Principal: Cesar Pelli
Collaborating Designer and Project Principal:
Rafael Pelli
Design Team Leader: Susana La Porta Drago
Designers: Robert Narracci, Fernando Pastor,
Victor Agran
Architect of Record
Beccar Varela
Structural Engineer
Alberto Fainstein y Asociados S.A
Curtain Wall Consultant
Peter M. Muller

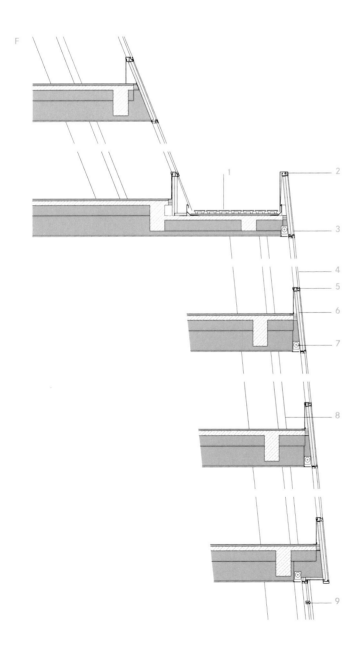

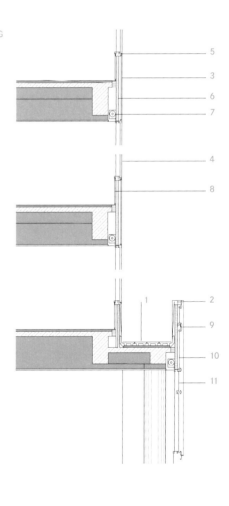

CHEUNG KONG CENTER
HONG KONG

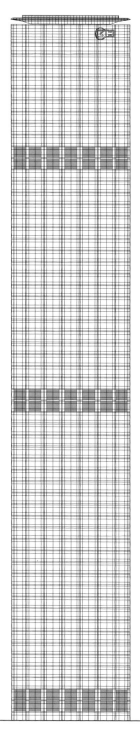

A

A
South elevation, scale 1:1500

B
Site plan

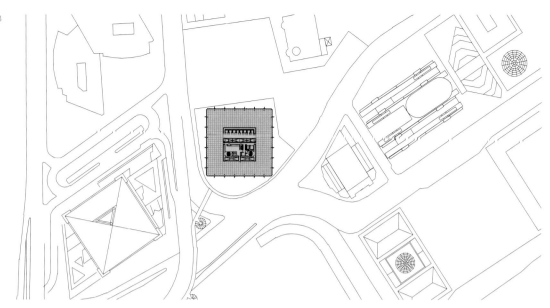

Context and Site: The site for the Cheung Kong Center is right between two large bank buildings: the Hong Kong and Shanghai Bank to the west and the Bank of China to the east. The design of the Cheung Kong Center was developed in response to two major project requirements: first, the local planning authority parameters for the height and massing of the proposed building in relation to its two prominent neighbors; and, second, the use of feng shui principles to determine the basic design of the building. The context of Hong Kong also demanded that the building be highly expressive in its lighting, so that it would have a presence on both the daytime and nighttime skyline of the city.

Architectural Form and Expression: The 280-meter building takes the form of a tall, elegant, and well-proportioned square prism. A feng shui master consulted on the project suggested the overall shape of the building, its square plan, orientation, and the need for a highly reflective curtain wall. The Hong Kong and Shanghai Bank and the Bank of China are both sculptured idiosyncratic forms, giving character to the skyline of Hong Kong. The form of the Cheung Kong Center does not attempt to compete with its neighbors; rather, it establishes its presence through its simplicity and elegance, and in contrast to these sculptural buildings. The crystalline reflective structure holds its own on the Hong Kong skyline.

Curtain Wall Components: The reflective glass wall is modulated by a wrapping grid of stainless steel lines. The corners of the buildings are slightly chamfered to accentuate the tautness of the building envelope and the surface continuity of the stainless steel grid.

Stainless steel is employed as the primary material because of its luminous character and its ability to reflect natural and artificial light. The horizontal divisions between the spandrel and vision panels are punctuated by brake-formed stainless steel fins that reflect both kinds of light and give the tower its strong layered texture (especially when illuminated at night). The vertical column covers that run the height of the tower are articulated as two engaged half-cylinders, which modulates their scale and provides a cleavage where the floodlights can be mounted.

Because the individual pieces of vision and spandrel glass are relatively large, 10mm-thick laminated glass is used for its strength and flatness. The glass is clear with a highly reflective sputter-coating of stainless steel, giving the material a silvery, dense finish that makes it hard to distinguish vision panels from spandrel panels.

At night, the dense pattern of light fixtures on the exterior of the building makes the tracery of the stainless steel grid glow, defining the prismatic quality of the building form. The floodlights mounted onto the stainless steel curtain wall column covers (arranged on an 8-meter grid vertically and horizontally) give the building a textural layer visible during the day. After dark, the floodlight evens out as it is visually dispersed through the stainless steel's linen finish (which gives the light thousands of corrugated surfaces to reflect on). A secondary, denser pattern of fiber-optic lighting is integrated into the curtain wall skin at the intersection of the panels. This fiber-optic system allows the building's illumination to change color and design during times of festivities. A bright edge of light crowning the top of the building further accentuates its form against the night sky.

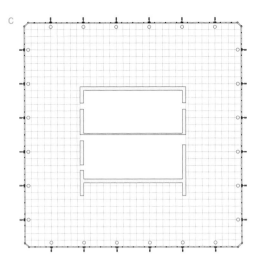

C

Night view from Star Ferry

Night view of east elevation

South elevation

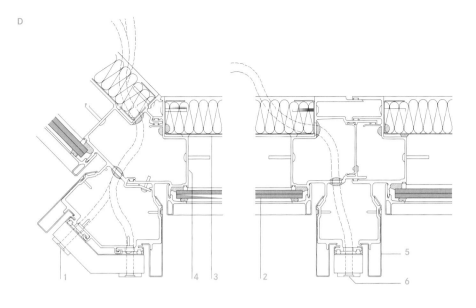

C
Typical mid-rise floor plan showing
concrete structure

D
Corner and vertical mullion detail
1 Fiber-optic light
2 Laminated spandrel glass with reflective
   coating, stainless steel finish
3 Insulated spandrel with metal shadow box
4 Custom extruded aluminum mullion system
5 Stainless steel with linen finish
6 Fiber-optic emitter lens

E
Section through uppermost levels showing
belt and outrigger trusses and roof feature
1 Uplit roof feature
2 Belt truss
3 Outrigger truss
4 Stainless steel
5 Bracketed uplight

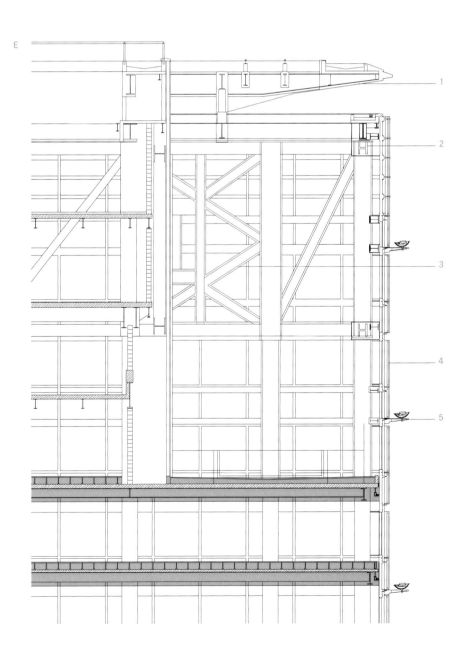

West elevation during curtain wall installation

Detail view of curtain wall and exterior lighting pattern

Curtain wall visual mock-up

Detail view of baffled uplight

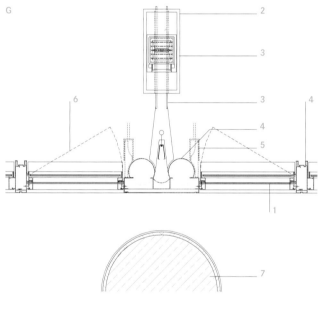

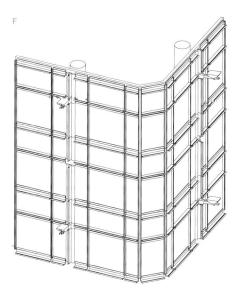

F

Location
Hong Kong, S.A.R.
Dates
1996–1999
Client
Cheung Kong Holdings Ltd. and Hutchison Whampoa Property
Building Program
Offices
Height
280 meters; 62 floors
Building Structural System
Concrete and steel
Curtain Wall Type
Unitized
Mullions
Stainless steel (#4 and linen finish)
Spandrel Panels
Reflective spandrel glass
Glass Type
Reflective vision glass

Lighting
Metal halide/fiber optics, integrated fiber-optic "stars", along with exterior wall mounted floodlight fixtures over the entire curtain wall
Curtain Wall Manufacturer
Permasteelisa
CP&A Project Team
Design Principal: Cesar Pelli
Collaborating Designer and Project Principal: Fred Clarke
Design Team Leaders: Jon Pickard, Mark Shoemaker
Project Manager: Lawrence Ng
Designers: Greg Barnell, Heather Coyne, Sascha Gerharz, Michael Hilgeman, Russell Holcomb, Yasushi Kikuchi, George Knight, Anthony Markese, Takahiro Sato, Heather Young
Associate Architect
Leo A. Daly
Structural Engineer
Ove Arup & Partners
Curtain Wall Consultant
Israel Berger & Associates

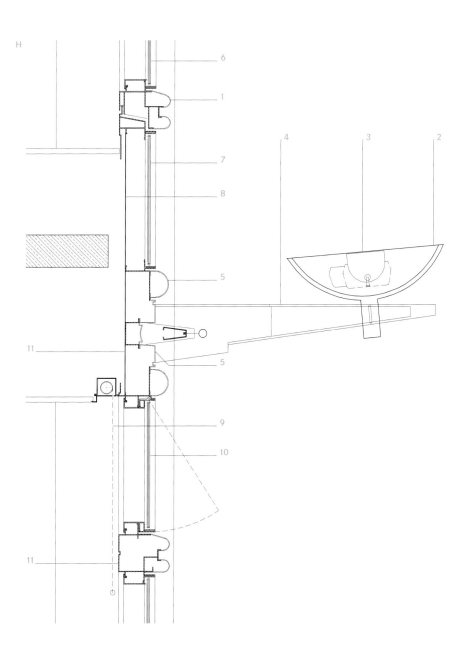

F
Axonometric showing chamfered corner condition

G
Plan detail at primary vertical mullion
1 Laminated spandrel glass with reflective coating, stainless steel finish
2 Baffled uplight on adjustable mount
3 Stainless steel #4
4 Linen stainless steel finish
5 Window washing track
6 Openable window
7 Concrete column

H
Typical wall section
1 Linen finish stainless steel mullion cap
2 Stainless steel #4 light scoop
3 Baffled light fixture on adjustable mount
4 Stainless steel #4 light bracket with stepped profile
5 Stainless steel
6 Laminated vision glazing with reflective coating, stainless steel finish. Structural silicone capture
7 Laminated spandrel glazing with stainless steel finish. Structural silicone capture
8 Metal back pan at shadowbox
9 Blind
10 Openable transom light
11 Custom extruded aluminum mullion

1500 LOUISIANA
HOUSTON

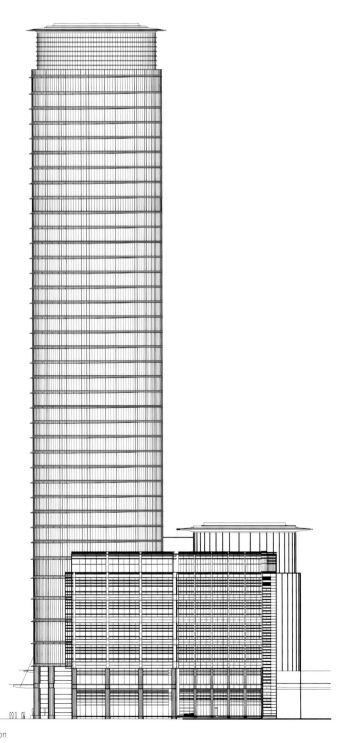

A

A
East elevation, scale 1:1000

B
Site plan

Context and Site: The client for this building conducted an invited architectural competition for the design of its new headquarters in downtown Houston, Texas. CP&A's winning design for the new 40-story south tower complements the company's existing 50-story north building.

The location of the new headquarters is at the periphery of downtown. The site and the existing building are skewed 55 degrees off of the downtown grid but aligned with the old city's layout of this area. In addition to similar orientations, the forms of the towers are also closely related, defining the company's campus as a distinct cluster of forms on the Houston skyline — an effect similar to the clustering of the Rockefeller Center towers in New York.

Architectural Form and Expression: Taking its cues from the existing building (and noting the client's preference for the proportion of the existing building's floor plan) the new tower is likewise lozenge-shaped. The new tower's massing is intersected with a seven-story podium, while the tower top is sculpted inward under a sweeping projected roof. The sunshaded texture of the new tower, coupled with the richly complex wall of the podium, distinguish it from the tradition of more taut, abstract building forms found in the city.

At the second-floor level is a circular bridge connecting the new and old buildings to each other and to a new parking garage. Designed structurally like an airplane wing, all the support for this bridge occurs within the deck, resulting in a transparent envelope. In a multi-story space at the juncture of the ring bridge and the tower is a five-meter-tall cylindrical map of the world, carved into 24 60cm x 550cm flat laminated glass panels hung in tension.

Curtain Wall Components: The exterior wall design of the new south tower has an elegant and environmentally responsive texture that helps to shade the building. The highly reflective skin of the new curtain wall is encircled by stainless steel bullnose ribs with a brushed finish running horizontally. As the bullnose moves around to the tower's south side, perforated sunshades gradually emerge from the metal band, projecting from just below the spandrel (the small perforations, at 60 percent of the surface, are the same lozenge-shape of the building). The 750mm-deep sunshades effectively reduce the amount of sun reaching the interior of the building.

Distinguished from traditionally more opaque building bases in Houston, the tower is visually open to pedestrians. The ground floor includes retail space, a 240-seat auditorium, and a two-story-high lobby with escalators leading to the second floor main elevator lobby. The lobby glazing consists of large panels of ceramic fritted, clear, low-emissivity glazing supported by four horizontal trusses hung from tension rods. Suspended delicate louvers provide sunshading and dappled light for the large lobby space.

The vision and spandrel glass for the tower has a high-performance coating containing chromium, which accentuates reflectivity (in fact, this is the most reflective glass that CP&A has ever used). The thin aluminum vertical mullions, virtually flush with the glass surface, are on 750mm centers and silicon jointed. At the tower's rounded ends the narrow glass width allows straight pieces to be used, yet the tower reads as a curved glass building.

C

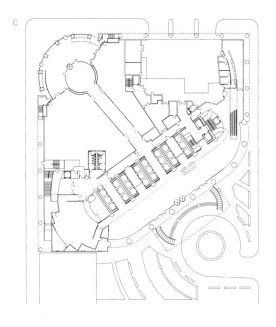

D

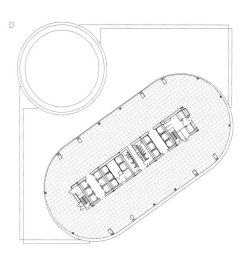

Rotunda and tower from below skybridge

South-west view of new and existing buildings

View down Smith Street of west elevation

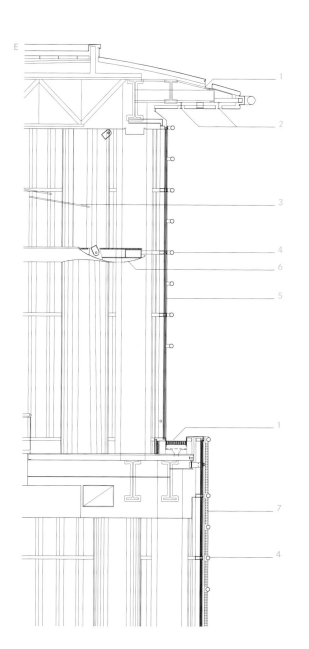

E

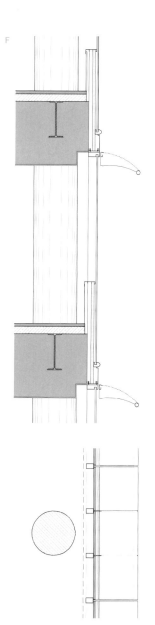

F

C
Ground floor plan with public lobby

D
Typical floor plan

E
Section through top of trading floor
podium rotunda
1 Gutter
2 Window washing rail
3 Perforated sculpted ceiling
4 Horizontal tubular sunshade
5 Graduated ceramic frit patterned
   insulated glass unit with 8% transmittance
   metallic coating
6 Lighting wing for sculpted ceiling
7 Perforated vertical blade sunshade

F
Tower south façade section and plan

G
Section through main lobby wall

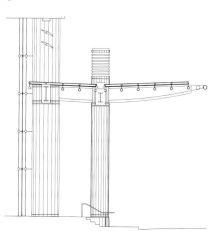

G

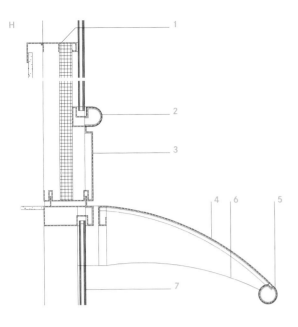

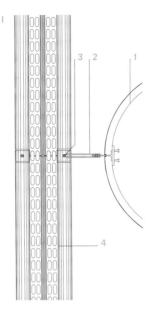

H
Tower south façade section
1 Sill
2 Aluminum bullnose
3 Aluminum spandrel panel
4 Perforated aluminum
5 Stainless steel clad pipe
6 Aluminum rib
7 Insulated glass unit with 8% transmittance metallic coating

I
Plan detail of main lobby wall
1 Exterior building column
2 Lateral stainless steel brace at each column 9.14m o.c.
3 Vertical stainless steel tension rods 3.05m o.c.
4 Horizontal perforated stainless steel truss 2.44m o.c.

Tower top

Tower under construction

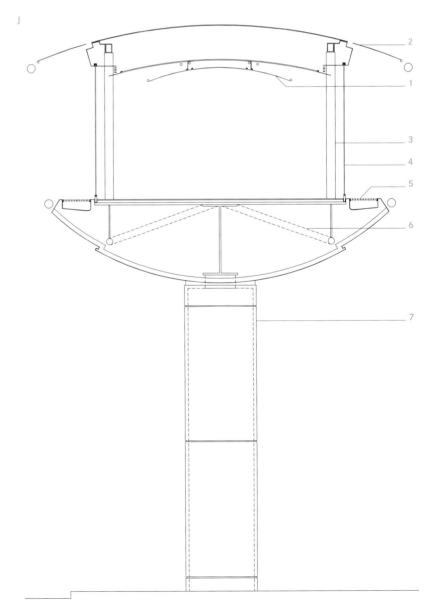

Location
Houston, Texas
Dates
1998–2001
Client
Hines
Building Program
Headquarters
Height
184.4 meters; 40 floors
Building Structural System
Steel moment frame braced by concrete core
Curtain Wall Type
"Semi-unitized" stick construction
Mullions
Extruded aluminum, with high performance coating
Sunshades
Painted outriggers and perforated aluminum with stainless steel tube
Spandrels
Tower spandrels are typical insulated glass units with ceramic frit. Podium spandrels are painted aluminum with concealed joints
Glass
Lobby glass is low-e with asymmetrically laminated units with ceramic frit
Lighting
Roof overhang has underlighting and twinkle lights. Lobby lighting gathered into linear ceiling troughs
Curtain Wall Manufacturer
Baker Metal Products
CP&A Project Team
Design Principal: Cesar Pelli
Collaborating Designer and Project Principal: Fred Clarke
Design Team Leader: Gregg Jones
Project Manager: Lawrence Ng
Senior Designer: Robert Narracci
Designers: Edward Dionne, Takahiro Sato, Gabriel Bekerman, Lori Bork, Tristan Dieguez, Barbara Endres, George Knight, Pablo Lopez, Dean Ober
Associate Architect
Kendall/Heaton Associates
Structural Engineer
CBM Engineers Inc.
Curtain Wall Consultant
Peter M. Muller

J
Section through skybridge
1 Continuous perforated aluminum lighting panel
2 Continuous perforated aluminum sunshade
3 Tubular steel roof support column
4 Laminated low-e glass
5 Gutter
6 Structure: circular truss, spine girder, and perimeter beam of plates and pipes
7 Exterior support column

K
Plan and section detail of main lobby wall
1 1.52 x 2.44m laminated glass panel, top and bottom capture, silicone vertical joints, low-e coating with graduated ceramic frit pattern
2 Vertical stainless steel tension rods 3.05m o.c.
3 Lateral stainless steel brace at each column 9.14m o.c.
4 Horizontal perforated stainless steel truss 2.44m o.c.
5 Exterior building column

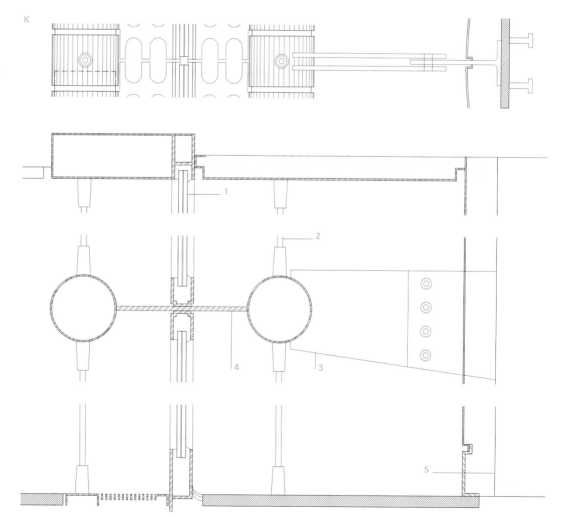

INTERNATIONAL FINANCE CENTRE
HONG KONG

A

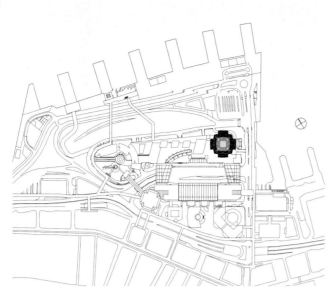

Context and Site: CP&A was selected by the Mass Transit Railway Corporation and the Central Waterfront Property Project Development Limited to design the new International Finance Centre after winning an international design competition. This project reflects the importance of Hong Kong as a world financial center and is part of a large complex of buildings. The 420-meter-tall tower occupies one of the most beautiful urban sites in the world, adjacent to the narrowest crossing of Victoria Harbor marking a new gateway to the city.

Architectural Form and Expression: The design of the tower is in the tradition of a true skyscraper, which Louis Sullivan described as "a proud and soaring thing." Its presence is simple, strong, and memorable. It is a great pylon or obelisk in the scale of the city and the harbor, visible from 360 degrees in every direction. Its centric form, which the observer can see on the skyline in its entirety from tip to toe, tapers with well-proportioned setbacks, expressing a vertical ascending movement. The massing of the tower, which also steps back at its corners, becomes more sculptural near the top, enhancing this upward thrust. It culminates in a crown that celebrates the height of the tower and its reaching to the sky. The crown's open design brings the blue of the sky into the tower's crown, partially dematerializing the building form as it reaches its highest point.

Curtain Wall Components: The surface articulation of the curtain wall reinforces the verticality of the design. The tower has setback corners, which makes the four sides appear as though they are "pillowed," bowing out toward the observer and the light. The vertical window mullions, which are painted aluminum, project out at a depth of 300mm, but are not very wide, and shaped like airfoils. When viewed from straight on they create a knife-edge impression and make the tower appear as a glassy pylon. As one moves around the tower, seeing it from oblique angles, the depth of the mullions is read, making this glassy wall appear less monolithic than it is. At the tower's setback corners the mullions are thinner, giving them a more glassy expression.

The paint for the metal components of the curtain wall was specially formulated. The City of Hong Kong is known as the "Pearl of the Orient," and the paint color is a pearlescent silver with a champagne tone. The paint is formulated with mica flakes, which give it its warm hue. The reflectivity of the paint was studied in conjunction with different sized mica flakes, the density of the flakes, how the finish would be applied and baked, and how it would weather. The result gives the tower its warm glow and reinforces the city's moniker.

The curtain wall is clad in lightly reflective vision glass panels. This choice is a middle ground between glass that is highly reflective and glass that has very low reflectivity. This also improves the clarity of the glass, allowing better color rendition for views from the tower. The spandrel glass is more reflective and has a white ceramic frit pattern applied to its inside surface which gives it a green cast. To make the ceramic frit read as truly white, it is slightly tinted with red (making it appear whiter when viewed through the glass). The frit pattern is very thin and delicate at the base of the tower, and becomes denser as the tower rises. The effect gives the International Finance Centre a strong, solid presence as it rises above the city.

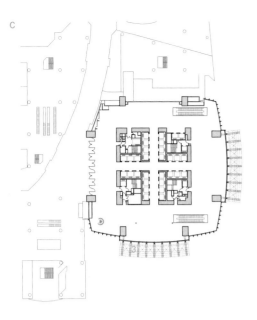

C
Tower entry and lobby plan

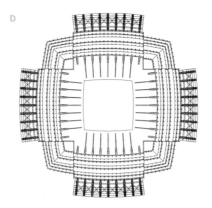

D
Tower roof plan

North-east view from Victoria Harbour

South-west view from Victoria Peak

View of corner from street level

E
Axonometric of exterior wall
1 Mechanical floor: 10mm heat-strengthened
   spandrel glass with reflective coating on
   #2 surface
2 Refuge floor: same as above
3 Exterior glass louver: laminated glass 300mm
   long, 60 degree angle with reflective coating
   on #2 surface with custom stainless steel edge
   support profiles. #4 brushed finish
4 Typical vertical mullion: two-part profile of bright
   white nose for inner sheath and silver pearl for
   outer sheath which decreases in size at each
   setback, revealing more inner bright white
   sheath. All components extruded aluminum
5 Vertical mullion at setback: extruded aluminum,
   bright white color
6 Typical spandrel glass: 10mm heat-strengthened
   glass with reflective coating and customized
   white ceramic frit pattern on #2 surface. Frit
   pattern increasing in density as tower rises

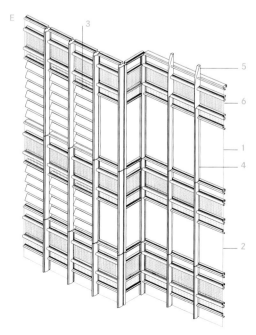

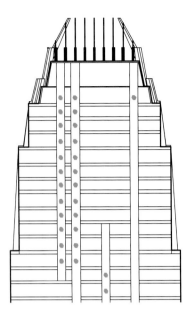

Street level view from within central district

Interior view of lobby mezzanine

North-west view from Victoria Harbour
of construction progress

F
Tower top section

G
Partial wall section at glass louvers
1 Exterior glass louver
   Laminated glass, 300mm long at 60 degree
   angle with reflective coating on #2 surface,
   stainless steel edge support profiles #4 finish
2 Horizontal mullion: extruded aluminum.
   Unitized panel stack joint with full internal
   guttering and air seal with 65mm accent
   tube, stainless steel #4 finish, mechanically
   fastened to bracket arms
3 Horizontal mullion: extruded aluminum
   with 120mm accent tube painted aluminum,
   mechanically fastened to bracket arms
4 Spandrel glass: 10mm heat-strengthened
   glass, with custom white ceramic frit pattern.
   #2 surface with reflective coating and 65mm
   deep shadow box, 1.2mm galvanized steel
   backpan with custom gray color

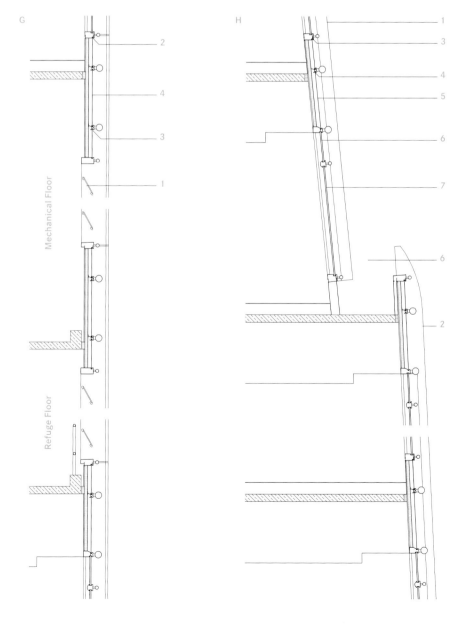

H
Section detail at sloping wall
1 6 degree sloping wall
2 3 degree sloping wall
3 Horizontal mullion: extruded aluminum.
   Unitized panel stack joint with full internal
   guttering and air seal with 65mm diameter
   accent tube, with stainless steel #4 finish,
   mechanically fastened to bracket arms.
4 Horizontal mullion: extruded aluminum with
   120mm diameter painted aluminum accent
   tube, mechanically fastened to bracket arms.
5 Typical spandrel glass: 10mm heat-strengthened glass, with custom color white ceramic
   frit pattern increasing in density as tower
   rises. #2 surface with reflective coating.
   65mm deep shadow box. 1.2mm
   galvanized steel backpan
6 Vision glass transom light: operable vent for
   emergency smoke evacuation, insulated
   glazing unit, 2–8mm heat-strengthened
   glass. Custom white ceramic frit pattern on
   #2 surface with reflective coating
7 Typical vision glass: insulated glazing unit.
   2–8mm heat-strengthened glass with
   reflective coating on #2 surface
8 1.2m setback: sloping walls between
   0, 3, 6 and 12 degrees

Tower top fins

Tower top under construction

I

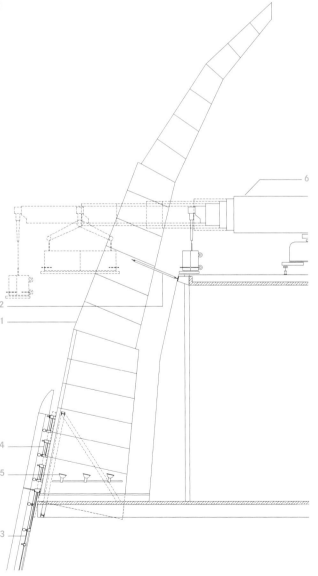

I
Tower top section
1 Roof fin accent feature: radiused panelized 3mm aluminum over galvanized steel armature 20m tall, aluminum splice joints, no sealant exposed
2 Structural bracket arm
3 12 degree sloping tower wall
4 12 degree sloping screen wall
5 Exterior spotlighting for fins
6 Telescopic gondola rig for building maintenance

J
Axonometric at tower top
1 3 degree sloping wall
2 6 degree sloping wall
3 12 degree sloping wall
4 Roof fins: exterior wall features 20m tall panelized radiused aluminum with white finish
5 Platform for building maintenance with telescopic gondola rig

J

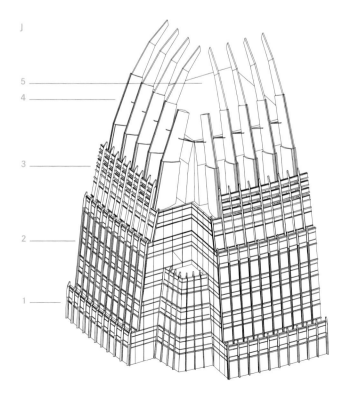

Location
Hong Kong, S. A. R.
Dates
1997–2004
Client
Central Waterfront Property Project
Management Company Ltd.
Building Program
Offices
Height
420 meters; 88 floors
Building Structural System
Concrete and steel
Curtain Wall Type
Unitized panel system
Mullions
Painted aluminum extrusions
Sunshades
Stainless steel and painted aluminum
sunshade accents

Spandrel Panels
Monolithic glass with reflective coating
and gradating custom ceramic frit pattern
in front of a painted aluminum shadowbox
Glass Type
Clear, insulated glass with a reflective coating;
custom ceramic frit pattern in the transom lite
Lighting
Vertical accent uplights, increasing in wattage
at each progressive setback and roof level
Curtain Wall Manufacturer
Permasteelisa
CP&A Project Team
Design Principal: Cesar Pelli
Collaborating Designer and Project Principal:
Fred Clarke
Design Team Leader: Gregg Jones
Project Manager: Lawrence Ng
Senior Designer: Edward R. Dionne
Designers: George Knight, Michael Hilgeman,
Martina Lind, Michael Koch, Dean Ober

Associate Architect
Rocco Design Limited
Structural Engineer
Ove Arup & Partners
Curtain Wall Consultant
Israel Berger & Associates
Arup Façade Engineering

K

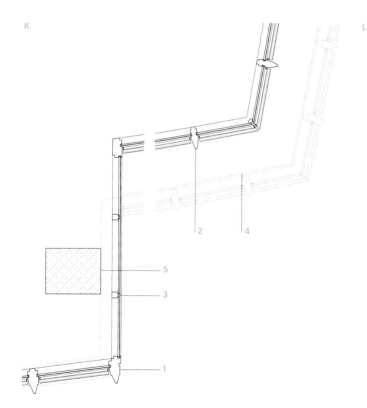

L

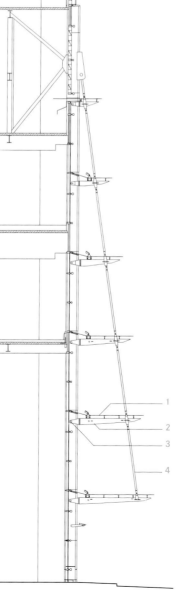

K
Partial plan detail at setback
1 Tower's primary face: 300mm projecting
   vertical profiles (extruded aluminum). Two-
   part sheath design: inner sheath is bright
   white, outer sheath is silver pearl
2 Tower's secondary face: 200mm projecting
   vertical profile
3 Tower's shear face: vertical is flush with
   glass surface
4 1.2m setback
5 Tower column: composite concrete and steel
   column

L
Section through entry canopy
1 Clear laminated glass with ceramic frit
   pattern, point-fitting attachment to
   steel rafter
2 Painted steel support rafter
3 Cast steel attachment arm, pin connection
   to vertical mullion profile
4 Painted steel compression strut
   160mm diameter

OVERTURE CENTER
MADISON

A
Fairchild Street elevation, scale 1:500

B
Site plan

A

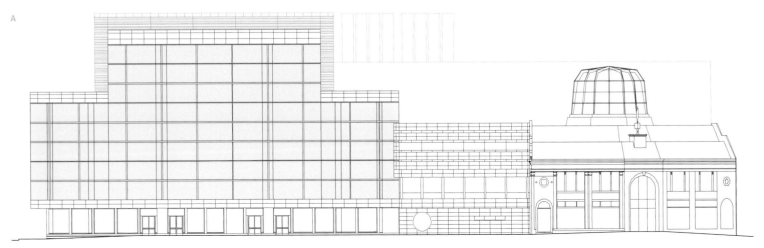

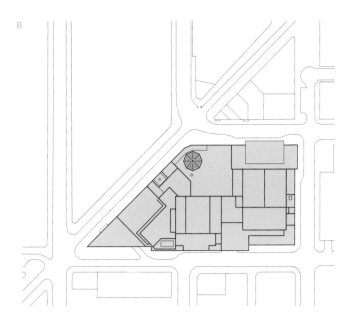

Context and Site: The Overture Center is part of a privately funded initiative to promote excellence in the arts and stimulate a downtown Madison, Wisconsin renaissance. Overture Center transforms the current Civic Center block, remodeling and expanding existing facilities and adding new ones. The most dramatic new public space at the Center – a glassy lobby for the new 2250-seat Overture Hall – is at the corner of Fairchild and Mifflin streets. This space is accessible directly from both of these avenues, as well as from the complex's main entrance – a glass-domed multilevel rotunda at the corner of State and Fairchild streets. The new glass curtain wall of the Overture Center welcomes sunlight from around the new concert hall to the east.

Architectural Form and Expression: The lobby's distinctive glass façade melds life on the street outside with lobby activity within, allowing theater goers to be "on stage" themselves as they move within this glowing, sparkling structure. The prismatic block of the glass lobby façade projects over the sidewalk to shelter the entrance and create a glowing, warm welcome, while providing a view back to the city and its lights.

Curtain Wall Components: The glass lobby curtain wall is supported with a series of structural steel mullions, which hang like a curtain from the beefed-up steel roof structure. The goal was to create a wall that was as transparent as possible, so the mullions and structure are detailed to minimize their appearance. Extending vertically from the roof structure are 750mm-deep fins that run from the ceiling to the floor of the space. These elements, which are clad in aluminum with an automotive paint finish, support the horizontal steel beams upon which the large pieces of glass rest. The fins also provide lateral support for the glass wall – thin metal struts tie back into the narrow end of the fins from the third points of the glass wall's

vertical mullions. To further suggest the dematerialization of the glass box, vertical structural elements are kept from the curtain wall's corners to allow them to be read clearly and without obstruction.

The horizontal steel sections supporting the glass are 300mm deep, clad in perforated aluminium, and include thin fin-tube heating elements to modulate the temperature of the glass wall. A sliding connection at the bottom of the wall allows for thermal expansion and contraction of the wall, and for deflections in the floor (which projects out over Fairchild and Mifflin streets).

Large pieces of glass – 6 meters wide by 3 meters high – accentuate the lobby's transparency. Each panel is made up of two pieces of 15mm glass with a 14mm airspace between them – weighing approximately 1225 kg per panel. To ensure absolute flatness of the panels, annealed glass is used because its fabrication process results in few deflections (annealed glass is floated on a bed of molten tin and does not pass through rollers, which can leave wavy lines on the glass surface). Low iron glass is specified because of its sparkling transparency, with virtually no tinting or reflectivity.

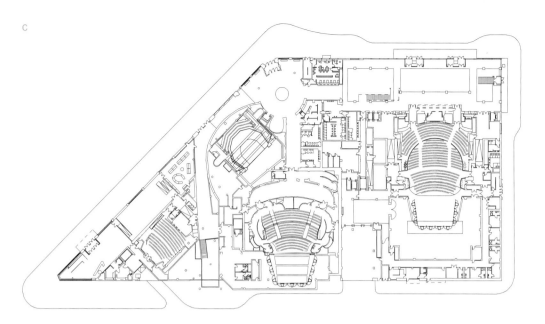

Overture Hall lobby from Fairchild Street

Night view of Overture Hall lobby

Overture Hall lobby

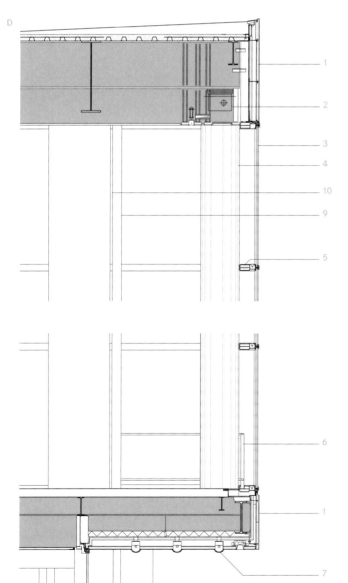

C
Ground floor plan

D
Detail section at Overture Hall lobby curtain wall
1 French limestone veneer
2 Steel hanging point for window column
3 Glass assembly
4 Typical window column
5 Typical horizontal mullion incorporating fin
   tube heating element
6 Stainless steel railing at base
7 Custom marquee architectural lighting
8 Stone soffit
9 Mullion beyond
10 Main structural column supporting roof

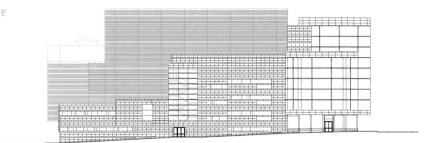

South-east elevation along Mifflin Street

Detail view of Overture Hall lobby curtain wall

E
Mifflin Street elevation

F
Axonometric view of structural steel design
and cladding profile at corner

G
Axonometric view of structural steel
design and cladding profile
1   15mm annealed low iron glass, 14mm
    airspace, 15mm annealed low iron glass
2   Exterior painted aluminum mullion cap
3   Fin tube heating element incorporated into
    horizontal mullion enclosure
4   Custom painted aluminum cladding,
    perforated band detail at fin tube
6   Clear anodized aluminum bar structurally
    bonded to glass lites
7   Custom painted aluminum cladding at
    structural window column
8   Structural steel connection
9   Stainless steel hanging rod
10 Steel tube clad in clear anodized aluminum

South-east corner of Overture Hall lobby

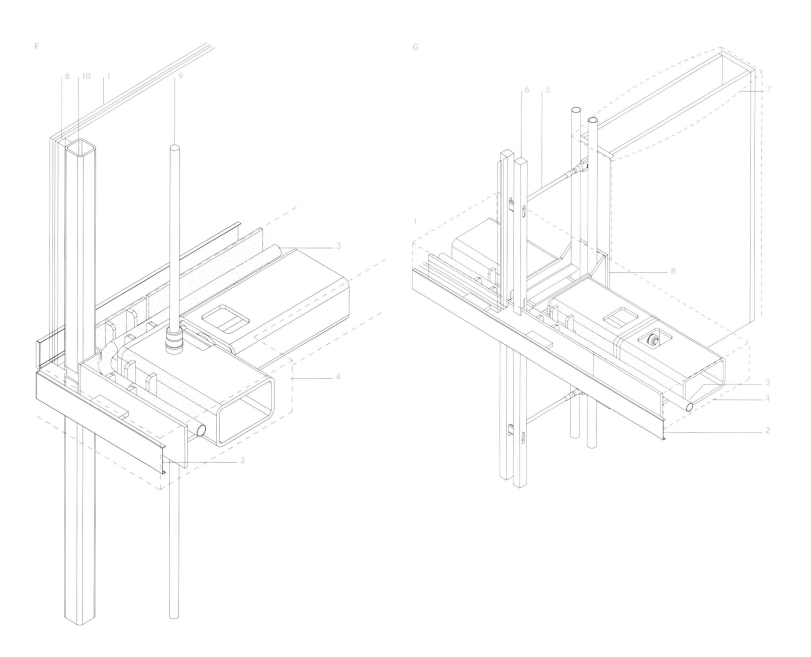

North elevation curtain wall installation

Interior detail view of Overture Hall lobby
curtain wall

Overture Hall lobby curtain wall visual mock-up

H
Plan detail at curtain wall perimeter

I
Section detail at horizontal and vertical
mullion interface

1 15mm annealed low iron glass, 14mm
   airspace, 15mm annealed low iron glass
2 Exterior painted aluminum mullion cap
3 Fin tube heating element incorporated into
   horizontal mullion enclosure
4 Custom painted aluminum cladding,
   perforated band detail at fin tube
5 Stainless steel support strut connecting from
   aluminum bar to structural window column
6 Clear anodized aluminum bars structurally
   bonded to glass lites
7 Custom painted aluminum cladding at
   structural window column
8 Structural steel window column connection
9 Custom painted aluminum cladding,
   rear face

Location
Madison, Wisconsin
Dates
1999–2004/2005
Client
Overture Foundation
Building Program
Cultural Arts Facility
Height
23.8 meters (top of rotunda)
Building Structural System
Steel and concrete composite; curtain wall
portion with steel core
Curtain Wall Type
Structurally glazed
Mullions
Custom shape aluminum cladding
Glass Type
Insulated low iron glass, two lites of 15mm
annealed glass separated by 14mm airspace
Curtain Wall Manufacturer
Mero Structures

CP&A Project Team
Design Principal: Cesar Pelli
Collaborating Designer and Project Principal:
Fred Clarke
Design Team Leader: William Butler
Senior Designer: Anne Gatling Haynes
Designers: Kara Bartelt, German Carmona,
Dominique Davison, Julann Meyers, Peter
Huang, Mai Wu, Barbara Endres, Philip Nelson,
Leonard Rehkop, Jonathan Fountain
Architect of Record
Potter Lawson & Flad, LLC
Structural Engineer
Thornton-Tomasetti Engineers
Curtain Wall Consultant
Israel Berger & Associates

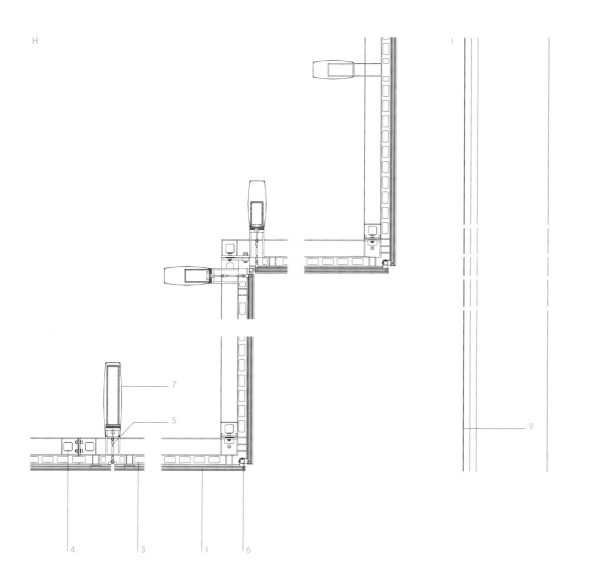

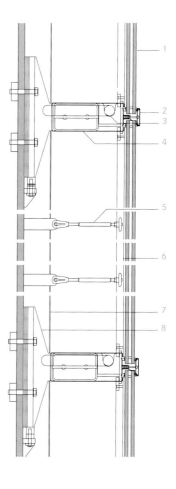

NATIONAL MUSEUM OF ART
OSAKA

A

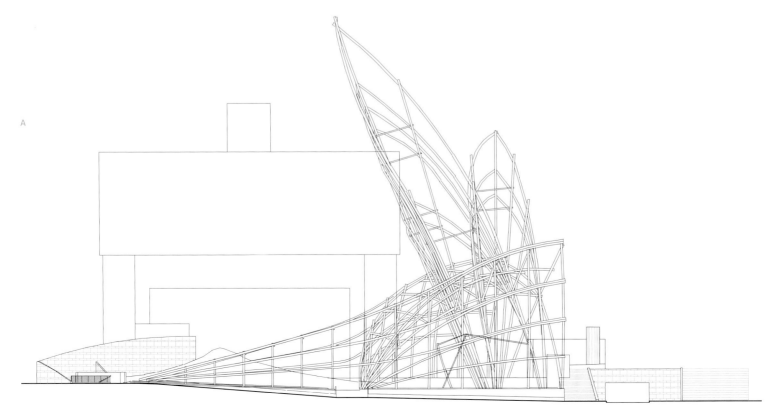

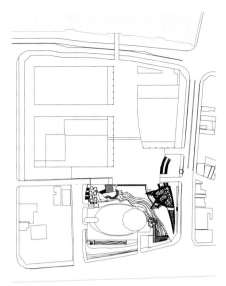

Context and Site: The National Museum of Art is located in the City of Osaka on the island of Nakano between the Tosabori and Dojima Rivers. Originally on the outskirts of Osaka, the museum relocated its collection of contemporary art to a gateway site in what is slated to become a major cultural and artistic district. The site is irregular and extremely tight, adjacent to an existing Science Museum, but it is in a magnificent location, a gateway to the Osaka Cultural Center. A key element in the city's revitalization, the museum creates a large plaza with places to exhibit and for people to meet and gather.

Architectural Form and Expression: The 13,500-square-meter building is on three levels, all below grade. The first level is the public free zone, followed by two levels of temporary and permanent gallery space.

While an agreement between the City of Osaka and the Ministry of Construction dictated that the entire building be built underground, CP&A was asked to give the museum a prominent and distinctive image, not only for itself but to announce the entire cultural center. The entrance is a sculptural form on an important view corridor within the city.

The design counterbalances the form of the existing Museum of Science and Industry which appears heavy, weighing down to the ground, while the National Museum of Art is very light, soaring in space, feeling as if it might wave in a slight breeze, like bamboo stalks bending in the wind. One building is solid, the other is transparent; one is made of surfaces, the other of lines. Together, they create a composition full of life.

Curtain Wall Components: The seemingly simple glass structure that marks the museum's entrance is actually quite complex and technically sophisticated. The total length of the tubular steel structure is 260 meters. It widens to 63 meters (north to south) and 40 meters (east to west). It rises to a height of 50 meters. Beneath this sculptural exoskeleton of stainless steel nests a steel truss structure painted industrial gray, which in turn helps to support the aluminum curtain wall that provides a weather-tight environment for the museum's entrance. This nesting of "a building within a building within a building" allows each to move somewhat independently to accommodate wind loads and potential seismic forces.

The brushed-finish stainless steel sculptural elements have a field-applied light catalyst titanium coating that causes water to bead up on the surface, keeping it dry, and makes the material self-cleaning so that airborne pollutants do not damage the metal and cause corrosion. The coating changes the appearance of the stainless steel, giving it a cooler, slightly bluish cast. The prosaic aluminum curtain wall system of 20mm mullions has a gray fluoropolymer finish, while the glass in the vertical walls is a clear, insulated, laminated-wire product with a low-e finish on its number 2 surface. The overhead glass panels have a white ceramic frit pattern to reduce solar glare.

Where a stainless steel stalk passes through the glass enclosure, it is fitted with a synthetic rubber bellows and a gasket for weather-tightness. Just below the bellows is an electrified stainless steel coil-woven sleeve that mitigates thermal bridging in cold weather, preventing condensation from forming inside the building.

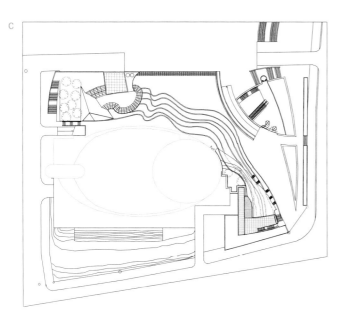

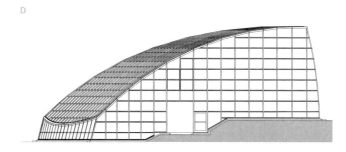

Main entrance

South elevation

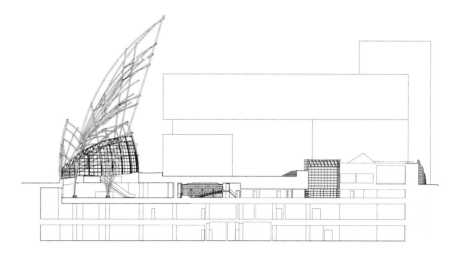

Night view of south elevation

C
Ground floor plan

D
Skylight elevation

E
East-west section

F
Model of sculptural form

F

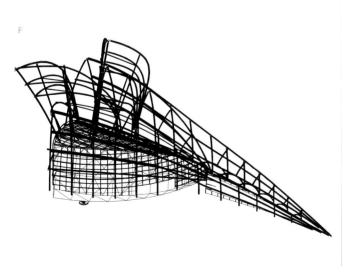

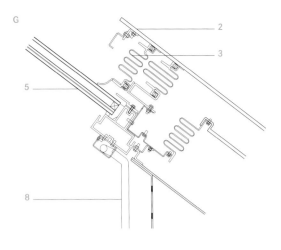

G

2

3

5

8

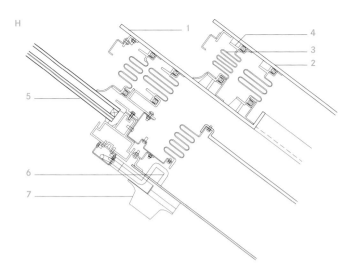

H

1

4

3

2

5

6

7

Atrium curtain wall

Interior view of atrium curtain wall

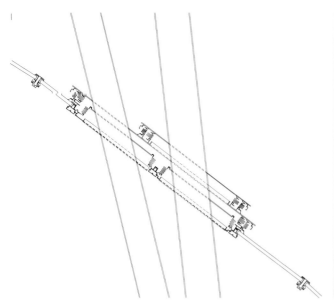

Detail view of atrium curtain wall and sculptural form

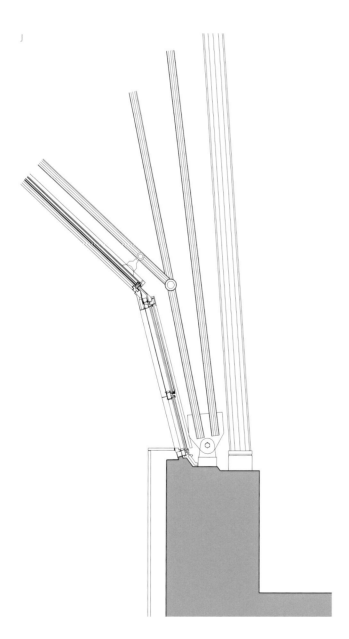

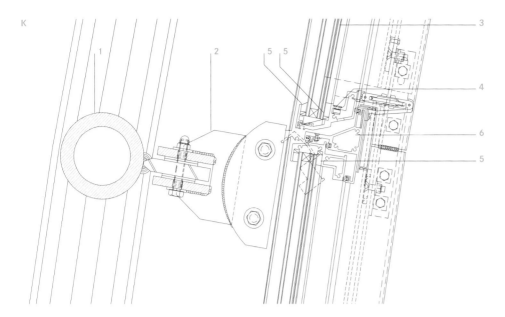

Interior view of atrium curtain wall

Detail view of stainless steel stalk base

K
Section through Skylobby
1 Steel pipe roof structure
2 Stainless steel gusset plate
3 Insulated safety glass
4 Condensation drainage valve
5 Silicon glazing seal
6 Drainage gutter

L
Section through internal gutter
7   Aluminum mullion
8   Aluminum gutter
9   Thermal break
10 Silicone joint sealant
11 Weep
12 Pre-molded rubber seal
13 High strength nut

M
Section detail of roller sunshade device
14 Aluminum closure panel
15 Stone coping
16 Steel base plate
17 Roller sunshade device

Stainless steel stalk passing through
atrium curtain wall

Location
Osaka, Japan
Dates
1996–2004
Client
**Ministry of Construction, Kinki Regional
Construction Bureau**
Building Program
Museum
Height
51.7 meters
Building Structural System
**Concrete and partially steel-framed reinforced
concrete**
Curtain Wall Type
Metal curtain wall
Mullions
Aluminum
Glass Type
**Double insulated laminated glass (wall);
double insulated glass with frit pattern (roof)**
Lighting
Halogen downlighting in public spaces

Curtain Wall Manufacturer
Fujisash Co. Ltd.
CP&A Project Team
Design Principal: Cesar Pelli
**Project Principal and Collaborating Designer:
Fred Clarke**
Design Team Leaders: Turan Duda, Keith Krolak
Project Manager: Lawrence Ng
**Designers: Gabriel Bekerman, Marla Lieberman,
Michelle LaFoe, Patricio Garcia, Paola Aboumrad**
Associate Architect
Cesar Pelli & Associates, Japan + JMA
Structural Engineer
Mitsubishi Jisho Sekkei, Tokyo

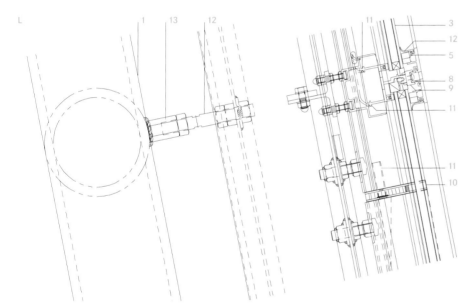

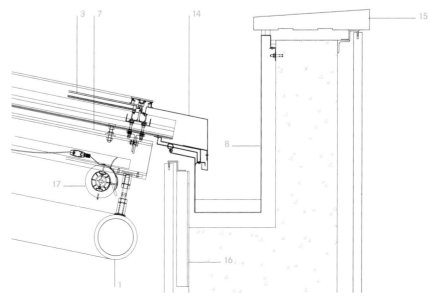

SCHUSTER PERFORMING ARTS CENTER
DAYTON

A
South elevation, scale 1:750

B
Site plan

A

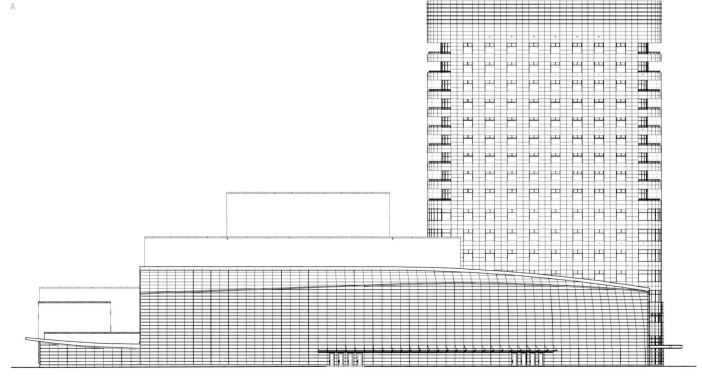

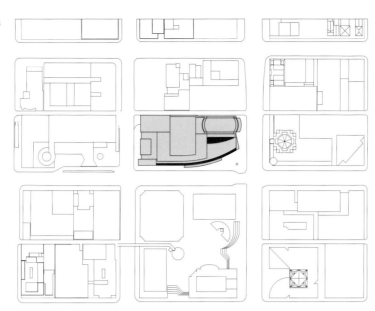

Context and Site: The site is a full city block in the heart of Dayton, Ohio, bounded by Main, West Second and Ludlow Streets, and West Booher Lane to the north. This location once housed the city's leading department store, which closed in 1992 and sat vacant for a number of years.

Architectural Form and Expression: The new complex consists of three components: a Performing Arts Center, an 18-story office/residential tower with below-grade parking, and a Winter Garden that serves to focus the entire ensemble. The Performing Arts Center accommodates a 2300-seat multi-purpose hall with a rehearsal/performance room and appropriate support facilities as the permanent residence for the Dayton Philharmonic as well as the Victoria Theatre Association and the Dayton Opera. It is also a venue for several local and regional arts groups.

The Winter Garden, a glazed public atrium, is the focal point of the complex around which all other elements are organized. The form of the Winter Garden is a compound curve, arcing in both plan and section. The shape suggests an aerodynamic wing, alluding to Dayton's place in history as the home of the Wright Brothers.

A descendent of the Winter Garden that CP&A designed for the World Financial Center in New York's Battery Park City, Schuster's Winter Garden serves as a lobby for the performing arts facilities and condominiums and as a forecourt for a restaurant and ticket office. Set well back from the intersection of Main and West Second Streets, it creates a generous public plaza and prominent entrance sequence, unifying the two ends of this long, narrow site. Its glazing continues to wrap the West Second Street façade, leading to a covered walkway over Ludlow Street to adjacent parking facilities.

Curtain Wall Components: The light-colored curtain wall with its clear glass gives the Winter Garden an uplifting sense of buoyancy while it commands this prominent corner site. The aerodynamically shaped sheath is supported inside by highly refined, lightweight steel trusses that arch over one's head like the limbs of graceful birch trees. The trusses are painted a soft green with a semi-glass finish, which adds sparkle to the surfaces.

The aluminum curtain wall is finished with a warm white epoxy semi-glass coating. The mullions measure approximately 20mm in width. Although the entire Winter Garden describes a gracefully curving structure, the curtain wall mullions are straight, canted at slight angles to accomplish the bowed appearance. The curtain wall modules are horizontal in their expression, 1.83 meters long and 60 cm high, reinforcing the sweep of the curve from one end of the site to the other. The curtain wall frame attaches to the steel trusses via horizontal sections spaced every five rows.

The insulated glass is very clear to accentuate views from the Winter Garden of the surrounding complex, and into the space from the neighborhood. The glass has a low-e coating to mitigate solar gain. A white ceramic frit pattern is applied to the number 2 surface of all the units, and helps the Winter Garden's form to be more easily read. The frit, rendered as polka dots approximately 2mm in diameter, has 40 percent opacity and helps to minimize glare in the space. The individual pieces of glass do not curve, but the canted curtain frame suggests that they do.

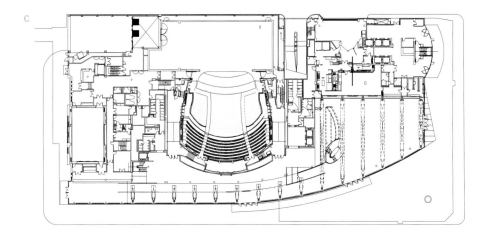

Winter garden from Second and Main Street

D

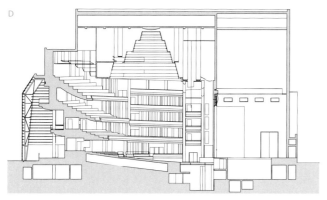

Winter garden curtain wall

Interior view of lobby/winter
garden curtain wall

C
Ground floor plan

D
North-south section through lobby and theater

E
Section at lobby

E

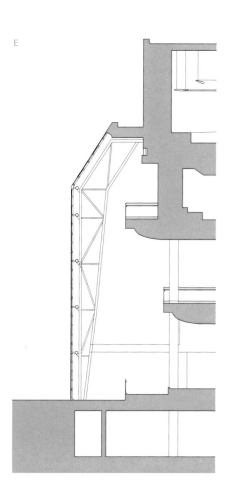

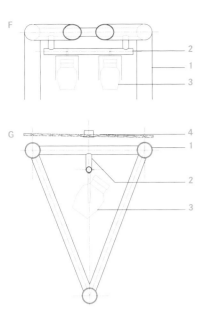

View west of wintergarden from Main Street

View from Main Street of wintergarden curtain wall under construction

Curtain wall performance mock-up

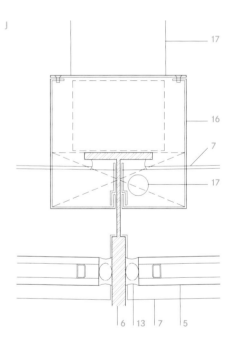

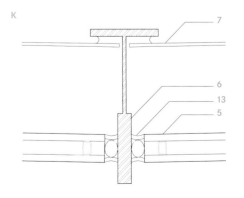

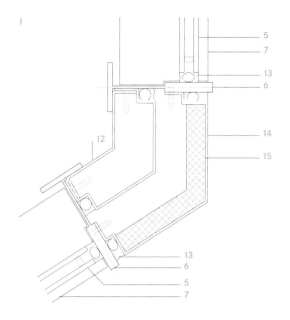

Location
Dayton, Ohio
Dates
1998–2002
Client
Second & Main Limited
Building Program
Performing arts center
Height
19.8 meters (wintergarden)
Building Structural System
Structural steel system with tube steel members
Curtain Wall System
Stick system
Mullions
Vertical mullions are continuous from base to top. Horizontal mullions are segmented between verticals.
Glass
25.4mm heat strengthened insulated glass with 40% ceramic frit and low-e coating. Glass sloped more than 15% and in the skylight is laminated.

Lighting
The curtain wall is lit from within the triangular trusses. Uplights in the plaza light exterior canopies.
Curtain Wall Manufacturer
Walter & Co Ltd.; Wintergarden trusses by SOFAB (Southern Ohio Fabricators)
CP&A Project Team
Design Principal: Cesar Pelli
Collaborating Designer and Project Principal: Fred Clarke
Design Team Leader: Mitchell Hirsch
Senior Designer: Gina Narracci
Designers: Seung Park, Andrew Nyhart, Olaf Recktenwald, J. Bunton, Bruce Davis, Kristin Hawkins, Julie Meyers, Marcela Staudenmaier, Alejandro Wasserman
Associate Architect
GBBN Architects
Structural Engineer
THP Limited, Inc.
Curtain Wall Consultant
Bob Baker

F, G
Section details at truss
1   Painted steel truss
2   50.8mm diameter light mounting pipe, painted
3   Light fixture and clamp
4   Linear wood ceiling system

H
Section detail at horizontal mullion and girt
5   25.4mm heat-strengthened insulated glass, low-e coating and 40% dot ceramic frit pattern silkscreen on #2 surface
6   Extruded vertical aluminum T-mullion, painted
7   Extruded horizontal aluminum mullion, painted
8   Painted steel girt
9   Slotted aluminum anchor plate
10 Bolt assembly, painted
11 Truss girt anchor support, welded to girt
12 Painted aluminum closure plate, sealed

I
Plan detail at south-east corner mullion
13 Structural sealant and backer rod
14 Painted aluminum exterior closure plate
15 25.4mm rigid insulation

J
Plan detail at vertical T-mullion
16 Painted aluminum junction box cover with top and bottom closure, with removable front cover
17 Fire alarm pull station with conduit running behind flange

K
Plan detail at vertical T-mullion

L
Section detail at horizontal beveled mullion
18 Painted aluminum square tube, continuous ice/snow guard bar
19 Painted extruded aluminum purlin

20 30.1mm laminated insulated glass, low-e coating and 40% dot ceramic frit pattern silkscreen on #2 surface
21 Painted extruded aluminum beveled mullion
22 Weep hole

M
Section detail at glass canopy
23 Painted aluminum downspout
24 Painted aluminum H-bracket
25 19mm diameter stainless steel bolt, lock washers and finish nut
26 1.9mm diameter stainless steel eye nut
27 1.9mm diameter canopy support rod with threaded attachment to eye nut
28 76.2mm diameter painted aluminum tube
29 Painted extruded aluminum T-section canopy strut
30 20.6mm laminated glass with custom frit pattern
31 Painted extruded aluminum T-section canopy intermediate cross member

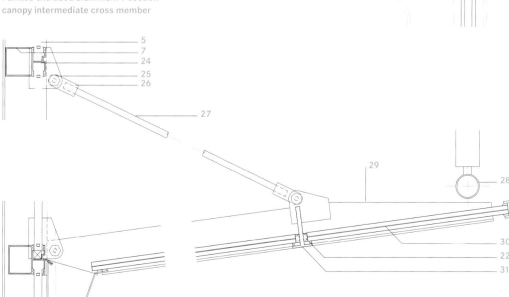

CIRA CENTRE
PHILADELPHIA

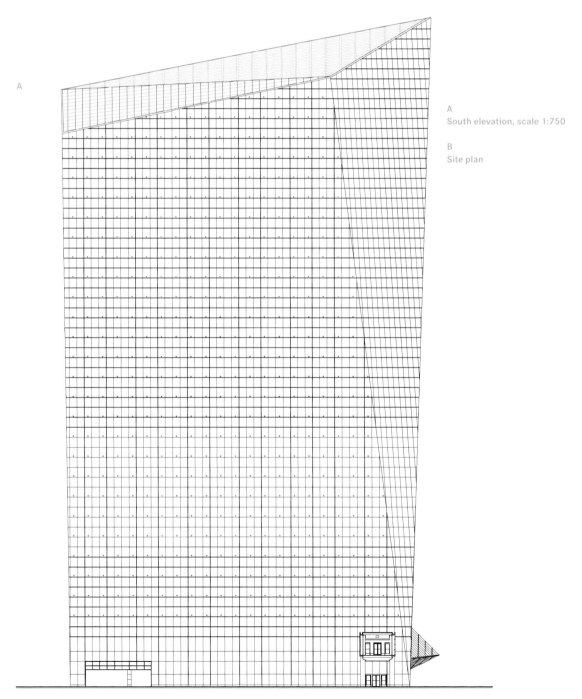

A
South elevation, scale 1:750

B
Site plan

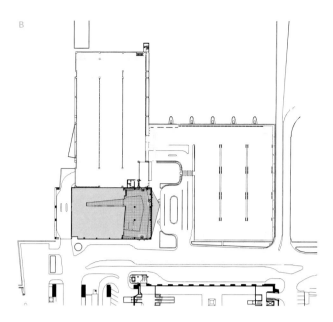

Context and Site: Cira Centre tower is situated in the air rights space over the railyards of Amtrak's 30th Street Station in Philadelphia. The project includes a grand foyer at the base of the tower that provides a link to Amtrak trains, SEPTA's commuter trains, and the parking garage. The 133-meter-high Cira Centre will replace the western third of the parking deck on Arch Street on the north side of the station.

In the larger context, the prism-like tower on Philadelphia's skyline will serve as a gateway for the region. The project is intended to expand Philadelphia's downtown across the Schuylkill River into a barren region occupied by the train station, the University of Pennsylvania, and Drexel University to make one urban complex.

Architectural Form and Expression: Because Cira Centre is in a part of the city that lacks urban density and offers full views of the building from several directions, it is meant to be read as a single, crystalline, sculptural object. This finds expression in the treatment of the building as a chamfered crystal, shaved at its corners to accentuate the tower's height. This esthetic treatment is also seen in the roof (which essentially becomes a folded wall angling up) and the base, whose tilted geometry spills out in front of the building. Formally, there is no distinction between the roof, the wall, and the entrance canopy — the surface is integral from tower top to bottom.

Curtain Wall Components: The focus of the curtain wall design is to support the formal reading of the building as a sculptural monolith on the skyline. This goal translates into a mullion system that is subdued in its expression, essentially two-dimensional in its graphic representation. The 75mm-wide mullions are rendered in brushed stainless steel, expressed as two thumb-thick bullnose fins that run horizontally but not vertically (in this direction the mullions are just proud of the

glass plane by about 25mm). This two-directional grid reads as a thin net on the building's surface, without an overt presence.

The genius of the mullion design becomes especially apparent at the entrance lobby, where the curtain wall comes straight down from the tower and then angles out to create a protective canopy. This is accomplished with a seamless surface transition — the mullions morph from being supported by the tower's structure to being a folded-plate structure. The support is provided by a steel-tube structural grid, 75mm wide, where the mullions rest upon its surface, and 150mm deep. The reading of the tower as a faceted object is preserved even at this close range.

The glass selected provides an integral reading of the tower's folded and tilted surfaces. Semi-reflective glass is used on both the vision and spandrel glass (the latter of which is configured as a shadow box, approximately 75mm deep, painted gray inside to mimic the reading of depth that one perceives behind the vision panels). The use of the same material across the building's surface essentially masks the distinction between vision and spandrel panels. At night, however, the spandrel panels are clearly expressed through the use of LED lights inside the shadow boxes, which animate the building's surface for an entirely different reading.

To achieve a consistent flatness for the insulated vision units with little distortion, 8mm glass is used for the outboard panel, while 6mm glass is used for the inboard panel, separated by a 13mm airspace. The glass is virtually clear, without tinting, to allow views of the outdoors from inside the building.

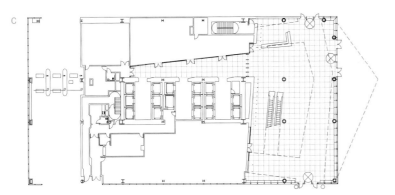

Rendering of east elevation

Entrance canopy visual mock-up

D

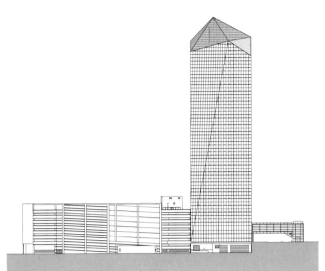

View from the Schuylkill River

E

C
Ground floor plan

D
West elevation

E
Section through lobby
1 Aluminum mullion with steel tube
   back support
2 Aluminum and low-e glass canopy
3 Ground floor
4 Amtrak track level
5 Second floor

F
Section at top floor

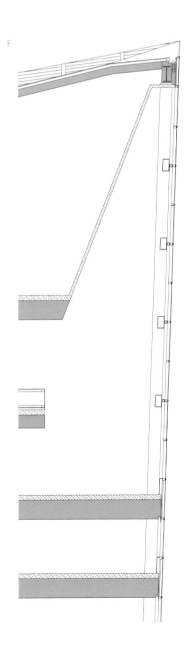

F

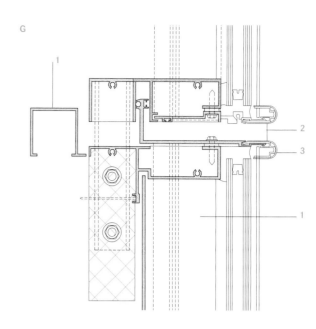

Canopy under construction

East elevation under construction

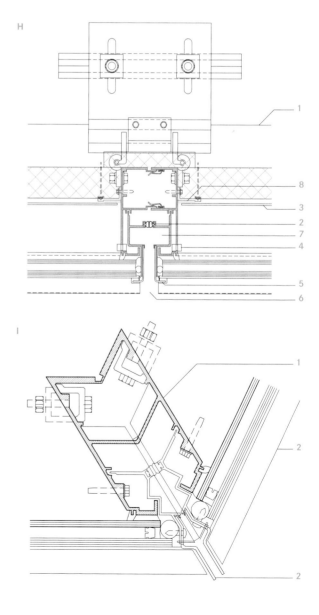

South elevation under construction

Location
Philadelphia, Pennsylvania
Dates
2002–2005
Client
Brandywine Realty
Building Program
Offices
Height
133 meters
Building Structural System
Steel structure
Curtain Wall Type
Unitized
Mullions
Aluminum with stainless steel cladding
Spandrel Panels
Shadow box with same glass and curtain wall system
Glass Type
Clear reflective low-e glass
Lighting
LED fixture in shadow box unit

Curtain Wall Manufacturer
Enclos Corp., Baker Metals Products
CP&A Project Team
Design Principal: Cesar Pelli
Collaborating Design Principal: Fred Clarke
Design Team Leader: Mark Shoemaker
Designers: Taek Park, Marla Lieberman, Joyce Hsiang, Mauro Vasquez
Associate Architect
Bower Lewis Thrower Architects
Structural Engineer
Ingenium, Inc.
Curtain Wall Consultant
Israel Berger & Associates

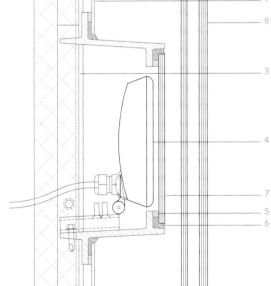

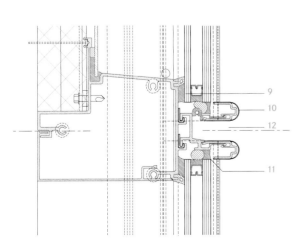

G
Typical horizontal mullion at stack joint
1 Shade pocket
2 19mm cavity
3 20 gauge stainless steel trim

H
Typical plan detail
1 Face of slab
2 Gasket
3 3mm aluminum panel
4 9mm vent hole with form baffle
5 Stainless steel trim
6 19mm cavity
7 Space for window washing rig roller mechanism
8 Structural silicone

I
Typical corner detail
1 Aluminum mullion
2 Stainless steel trim

J
Typical section detail at shadow box
1 3mm aluminum panel
2 Insulation
3 Insulation filled in after installation of light fixture
4 LED fixture
5 Double face tape
6 Structural sealant
7 Sealed clear glass lens
8 Low-e reflective vision glass
9 Structural silicone
10 20 gauge stainless steel trim
11 Silicone and backer rod
12 19mm cavity

CENTRAL LIBRARY
MINNEAPOLIS

A
East elevation, scale 1:500

B
Site plan

A

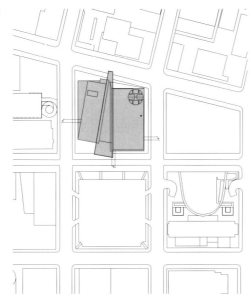

Context and Site: Located at the north end of Nicollet Mall, the new Central Library is a vital civic landmark and cultural center for downtown Minneapolis and the region. The new building houses the state's largest public library collection of printed and electronic media. The new library is a dynamic, resource-rich downtown destination, conveniently located between Hennepin Avenue, with the arts and theater district to the west, and Nicollet Mall, the backbone of the city's business and shopping districts.

Architectural Form and Expression: The shifting urban geometry carries through the public space of the low-rise building. Above the resulting space between the library's two main building blocks floats a wing-like roof that spans over the Nicollet and Hennepin entrances. Under the sculptural roof, the five-story, glass-enclosed Library Commons, flanked by plazas on Nicollet and Hennepin, becomes the "living room" for Minneapolis.

Curtain Wall Components: Dramatic curtain walls are found at the building's front and back, as it faces Nicollet (under the wing roof) and on the opposite side overlooking Hennepin Avenue. These two curtain walls enclose the Library Commons on its east and west ends. On the wider east side, a delicate steel and stainless steel hanging structure supports the glass units, which measure 2.74m high by 4.88m wide and are set on horizontal stainless steel pipes circulating hot water for radiant heat. The curtain wall system, suspended from the roof structure, includes a series of steel frame bridges linking the north and south wings at the east end of the galleria. The bridges provide lateral support to the curtain wall and transfer the gravity load of the glass to steel tension rods. The narrow west curtain wall is supported by thin stainless steel columns.

The low iron, low-e glass units have 15mm outer and inner lites, with a 12mm argon-filled cavity between them.

The library's two wings read as a series of slab-like floors, interspersed with lively layers of expressive glass. The library's concrete structure is suggested in the slabs that extend out beyond the curtain wall's glass line. The slabs are clad in a honed, golden Minnesota Stone, mounted on 150mm precast concrete panels approximately 600mm high.

As a counterpoint to this native, ancient material, the ribbon windows that wrap the building are contemporary yet just as expressive of nature. The glass plane shifts in and out approximately 100mm, breaking up the solidity of the curtain wall and giving the building a texture of fenestration. The floor-to-ceiling units are double-pane, high-performance glass in thermally broken, clear-anodized aluminum mullions. Low iron glass achieves crystal clarity and a strong visual connection between inside and outside.

The glass has a sophisticated white ceramic frit design on all four sides of the building, responding to the context and the environment. The frit is densest on the south elevation to block heat gain; to the north it is more sparse. The ceramic frit is applied on number 2 surface of the double-pane units. From up close the frit appears to be a random pattern of 32mm pixel squares, but as one views the patterns from across the building or across the street, images emerge. On the Nicollet façade, the frit patterns describe an abstract forest of white birch trees, their trunks beginning on the ground level with their branches dividing as they reach the top floor. On the side of the library that faces the Mississippi River, the frit pattern suggests the surface of water. Other patterns include prairie grass and snow. All of the images are derived from photographs of Minnesota landscapes. The fritted curtain wall modulates the sun, helps reduce glare, and also tells the stories of the building's region.

C

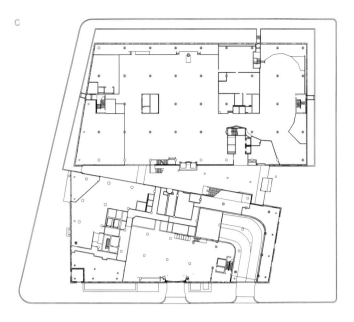

D

Rendering of east elevation

E

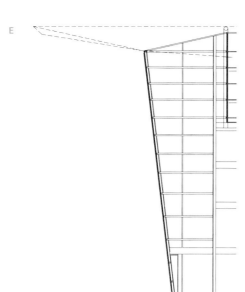

West elevation under construction

F

F

Nicollet Avenue bridge section

1   Steel tension rod
2   Finished floor over concrete deck
3   Cantilevered glass guardrail
4   Structural steel frame
5   Steel hanger frame
6   Stainless steel pipe with hot water circulat-
    ing through it
7   2.74 x 4.88m insulated low iron glass units
    with low-e coating
8   Pivoting tie connector
9   Tapered and bolted connection between
    steel hanger frame and stainless steel pipe
    with teflon pads
10 31.8mm aluminum frame, structurally
    adhered to back surface of glass units
11 Pressure plate assembly with continuous
    stainless steel cap

G

Plan detail of Hennepin Avenue curtain wall

1   152.4mm diameter stainless steel pipe with
    hot water circulating through it
2   88.9mm diameter stainless steel
    pipe column
3   12.7mm stainless steel plate
4   31.8 x 31.8mm anodized aluminum bar stock,
    structurally adhered to glass
5   Stainless steel jam nut
6   44mm insulated low iron glass with low-e
    coating on #2 surface
7   Grey silicon sealant with 17.1mm closed
    cell backer rod
8   6.4 x 31.8mm aluminum bar accent strip,
    forward face set coplanar with outside face
    of glass
9   6.4mm glazing tape with silicone sealant
    at edges
10 22.2mm diameter 11 gauge wall stainless
    steel tube

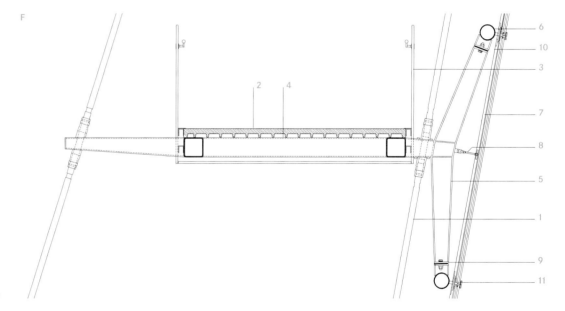

G

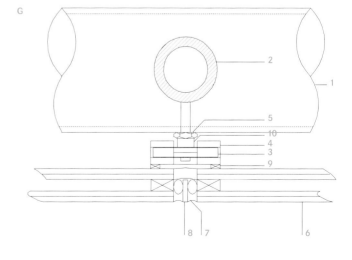

Typical fritted window wall (prairie grass pattern)

Typical fritted window wall (birch tree pattern)

Rendering of north elevation

Interior view of typical fritted window wall
(Minnesota lakes pattern)

Location
Minneapolis, Minnesota
Dates
2001–2007
Client
City of Minneapolis Library Board
Building Program
Library
Height
32 meters above grade on northern edge
Building Structural System
Poured in place concrete structure
Curtain Wall Type
Semi-unitized split mullion
Mullions
Stainless steel curtain wall components
Sunshades
Automated Mechoshade system behind wall
Spandrel Panels
Minnesota stone
Glass Type
Low iron glass with a low-e coating
Three types of window panels: Clear glass with

pinstripe frit lines; translucent fritted glass;
fritted glass with reflective coating and opaque
metal back panels
Curtain Wall Manufacturer
HKL (enclosure); Mero Structures;
Eckelt/St.Gobain (Glass)
CP&A Project Team
Design Principal: Cesar Pelli
Collaborating Design Principal: Fred Clarke
Design Team Leader: William Butler
Designers: Elijah Huge, Aicha Woods, Sebastian
Mallea, Julie Meyers, Jose Luis Cabello, Paul
Aroughetti, Rafael Barona, Dustin Eshenroder,
Luciana Lins de Mello, Emily Kirkland, Karin
Patriquin, Robert Riccardi
Associate Architect
Architectural Alliance
Structural Engineer
Thornton-Tomasetti Engineers
Curtain Wall Consultant
Israel Berger & Associates

H
Detail 1
Right: Clear unit, glass set forward
Left: Clear unit, glass set back

I
Detail 2
Right: Opaque unit, glass set forward
Left: Opaque unit, glass set forward

J
Detail 3
Right: Clear unit, glass set back
Left: Opaque unit, glass set forward

1   50 x 200mm thermally broken clear-anodized
    aluminum mullion
2   Extruded grey silicone gasket
3a 25mm low iron insulated glass unit with
    low-e coating and white ceramic frit on #2
    surface. Glass set in forward position
3b 25mm low iron insulated glass unit with
    low-e coating and white ceramic frit on #2
    surface. Glass set in back position
4   100mm rigid insulation
5   3mm aluminum closure panel, painted white
6   intermediate horizontal mullion (below)

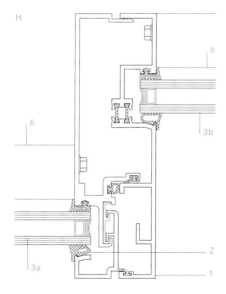

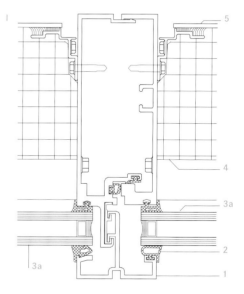

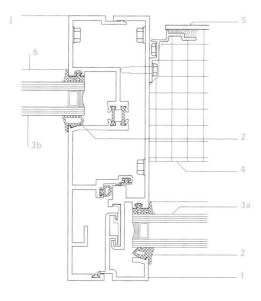

TORRE DE CRISTAL
MADRID

A

A
South elevation with curtain wall zones
scale 1:1250

B
Site plan

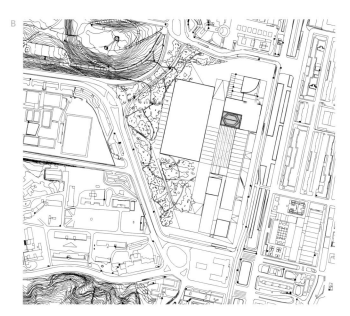

B

Context and Site: The four towers of the development Ciudad Deportiva del Real Madrid constitute a group of what will be the most important buildings in Madrid (and in all of Spain). Although the towers form a group, they are sufficiently separated to be seen individually as vertical sculptures against the sky. Torre de Cristal is Pelli's contribution to the quartet of towers, designed for the client Mutua Madrileña Automovilista.

The design of the Torre de Cristal expresses the optimism and the dynamism of the new Madrid. The tower appears as a sculpture chiseled out of a great block of crystal, its facets capturing the light of the sky as if it were a carved diamond. As a result of the variety of the angles of its facets, some of them will always reflect the light of the sky more strongly, giving great life and movement to the total form.

Architectural Form and Expression: The shape of the tower has a very old lineage that perhaps begins with the obelisks of Egypt but, at the same time, has a contemporary presence full of life. The tower seems to rise from the ground with great force and aim towards the sky, accentuating its verticality. The observer's eyes are taken from its base to its top. Torre de Cristal terminates with sloping facets in a gesture of reverence towards the sky. It will immediately be a recognizable and unforgettable form in the skyline of Madrid.

At night, the winter garden, at the top of the tower, becomes an immense source of light visible all along the Paseo de la Castellana and from all the North area of Madrid.

Curtain Wall Components: The esthetic function of the curtain wall is to support the reading of the tower as a crystalline object, and the system is designed to accentuate the surface continuity of the wall. For example, the curtain wall's horizontal module is 2.4 meters, which results in larger pieces of glass than the more standard 1.5-meter module;

as a result, the glass openings read more as "picture" windows. The glass chosen needs to have a minimum of surface distortion (which would detract from its reading as a crystalline tower) and must support the building's thermal performance (which is demanding – summer temperatures sometimes reach 39 degrees Celsius).

A high-performance double-pane insulated material is used that combines the thermal characteristics of low-e glass with minimum reflectivity and greater transparency. A second layer of single-pane glass is positioned inboard from the exterior glass to achieve a ventilated double wall. The gap between the two glass panels is approximately 220mm. The inboard glazing is laminated so that it can resist horizontal impact loads. In the winter garden at the building's top, the ventilated double wall is not used, and the roof is clad with the double-pane insulated units.

The entire tower employs the same curtain wall mullion system composed of narrow-profile aluminum components that are in the same plane as the glass surface. The aluminum has a natural anodized finish that was chosen for its low luster – the mullions have a subtle presence to allow the glass surfaces to read without the glint of metal reflections. The same mullion system is used on the roof surfaces and at the building's lobby to provide a uniform reading of the curtain wall throughout. The tower is scheduled for completion in 2008.

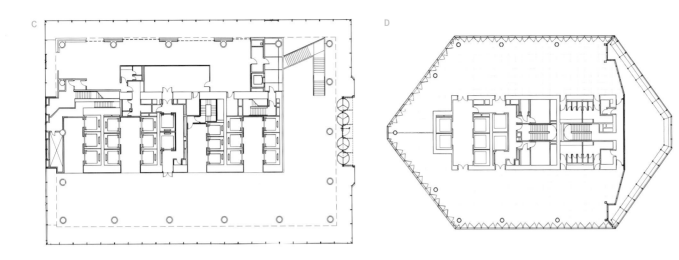

Rendering of view from Paseo La Castellana

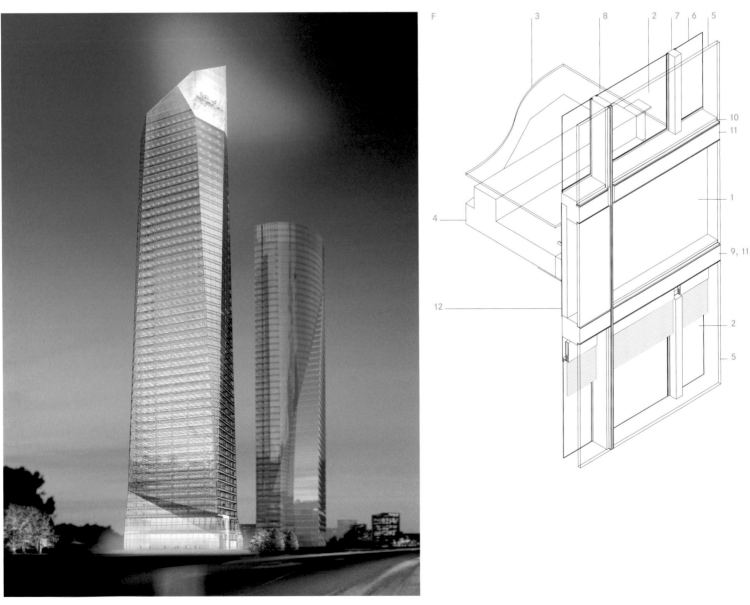

E

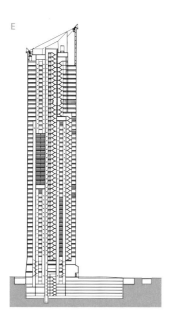

Location
Madrid, Spain
Dates
2003–2007
Client
Mutual Madrileña Automovilista
Building Program
Offices
Height
250 meters
Building Structural System
Concrete core building system with steel framing and composite (steel and concrete) columns
Curtain Wall System
Unitized
Mullions
Painted aluminium profiles with anodized aluminium cover on the outside
Spandrel Panels
Sealed double glazing unit with a high-performance coating on #2 surface
Outer lite: single heat-strengthened glass;

inner lite: laminated heat-strengthened glass
Glass Type
Sealed double glazing unit with a high-performance coating on #2 surface
Outer lite: single annealed glass; inner lite: laminated annealed glass
CP&A Project Team
Design Principal: Cesar Pelli
Collaborating Design Principal: Fred Clarke
Design Team Leader: Lawrence S. Ng
Designers: Javier Roig, Axel Zemborain, Susana La Porta Drago, Anibal Bellomio, Alejandro Scarpa, Joyce Hsiang
Associate Architect
Ortiz León Arquitectos
Structural Engineer
Otep International, S.A.
Curtain Wall Consultant
Emmer Pfenninger Partner AG, Switzerland

C
Ground floor plan

D
Floor plan level 46

E
West-east section

F
Axonometric of typical curtain wall module
1   Shadow box
2   Vision glass area
3   Raised floor
4   Structural slab
5   Sealed double glazing unit
6   Interior operable laminated glass panel
7   Intermediate mullion, painted aluminum profile (powder coat) pearl light gray matte finish
8   Panel joint mullion, painted aluminum profile (powder coat) pearl light gray matte finish
9   Air intake per floor
10 Curtain wall panel stack joint
11 Natural anodized aluminum
12 Painted aluminum sheet (powder coat) silver gray, matte finish

G
Plan detail for typical corner
1   Composite concrete and steel column
2   Sealed double glazing unit
3   Intermediate mullion painted aluminum profile (powder coat) pearl light gray, matte finish
4   Panel joint mullion painted aluminum profile (powder coat) pearl light gray matte finish
5   Aluminum blinds 25mm wide, with a 50% minimum reflectance value
6   Interior operable laminated glass panel
7   Interior operable laminated glass panel with custom ceramic frit to mimic blinds
8   Edge of structural slab below

H
Typical curtain wall section
1   Shadow box area
2   Vision glass area
3   Air intake/exhaust per floor
4   Stack joint
5   Sealed double glazing unit
6   Blind pocket, painted aluminum (powder coat), silver gray matte finish
7   Aluminum blinds 25mm wide, with a 50% minimum reflectance value
8   Sealed double glazing unit with a high-performance coating on #2 surface
9   Interior operable laminated glass panel
10 Curtain wall air cavity intake
11 Curtain wall air cavity return
12 Painted aluminum sheet (powder coat) silver gray matte finish
13 Rock wool
14 Fire rated panel
15 Natural anodized aluminum
16 Painted aluminum profiles (powder coat) pearl light gray matte finish

G

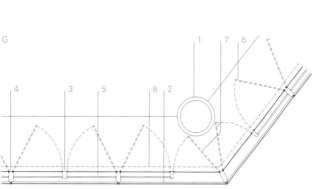

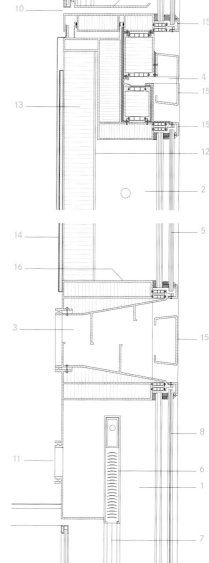

CITIGROUP TOWER
LONDON

A

A
East elevation, scale 1:1000

B
Site plan

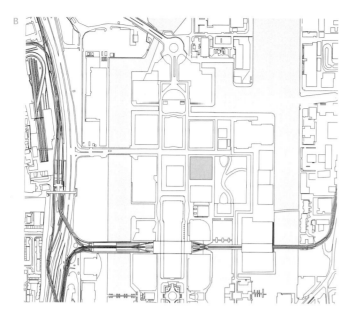

Context and Site: The 42-story, 200-meter-high Citigroup headquarters tower adjoins Norman Foster's building for Citibank (the firm has designed approximately a dozen buildings in London's Canary Wharf development). The tower provides an esthetic link to the 48-story landmark One Canada Square Tower designed by CP&A as the first project in the development, and the 42-story HSBC tower. The three towers together, with a retail center and a park connecting them (as originally master planned), aggregate more than 325,500 square meters of commercial space.

The corporate and investment banking businesses of Citigroup occupy 55,800 square meters within the new building, creating a combined Citigroup complex of 107,880 square meters for 6000 Citigroup staff.

Architectural Form and Expression: The tower has a centric composition that gently tapers toward the top. The façade's super-grid enhances the tower's formal order and aligns with the super-grid of the adjacent Citibank building designed by Foster and Partners to form a common building base. The tower top is crystalline and transparent, offering a crowning gesture when lit at night.

Curtain Wall Components: The choice of materials for the curtain wall responds to the context of the earlier buildings. In comparison to the earlier tower, Citigroup's curtain wall is more open and transparent. The 10-meter structural grid is expressed by wide column covers in a brushed-finished stainless steel that accentuate the tower's height. The elements contain the tracks for the window-washing mechanism. This module is halved by a narrower stainless steel column cover with a curved surface that splits the bay into two window openings.

Wide stainless steel spandrel panels populate the lower third of the tower, banding it at every third floor. The curtain wall then shifts gears and the spandrel panels become narrower and alternate with shadow box spandrels. Thin rods of brushed stainless steel overlay the windows' vertical mullions and provide another layer of highlights. At the very top of the tower, a glassier curtain wall emerges from the core, with stainless steel spandrel and column covers that are thinner than those seen in the building's lower floors. The curtain wall design also contributes to the reading of the building as lighter and less solid, thanks to the glass corners on each floor where the tower is recessed (recalling a similar recess on Canary Wharf Tower). This detail, along with the spandrel glass line at the very top of the building, suggests a thin skin, as it appears to wrap the tower's form.

The glass used throughout the tower is a sealed, double-pane unit with a high-performance coating on the number 2 surface that achieves a shading coefficient of 0.37, which helps to cut heat gain. The glass has a reflective quality to it, and the color is slightly green, which unifies the entire curtain wall surface vision glass and spandrel glass panels.

C 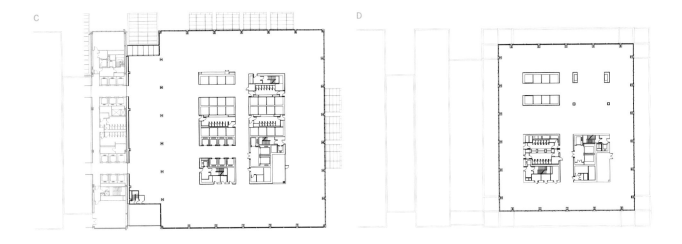 D

Detail view of corner setback

C
Floor plan level 2

D
Floor plan levels 41–42

E
Exterior and interior corners of typical
curtain wall showing supergrid

F
Section through typical curtain wall

View of tower setbacks

East elevation

View of curtain wall from Jubilee park

E

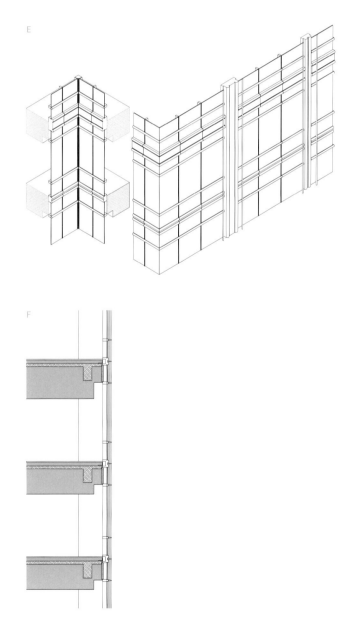

F

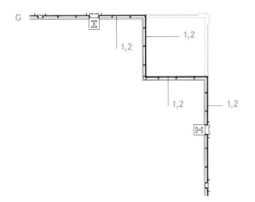

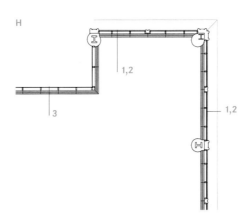

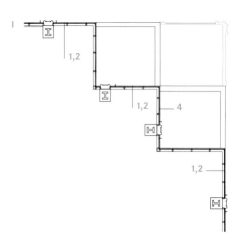

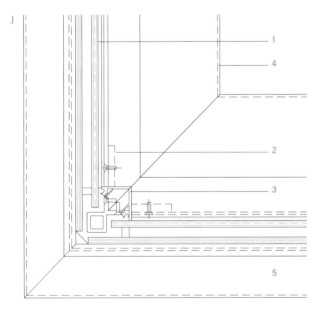

G
Corner detail level 24–35

H
Ground lobby corner detail

I
Level 36–40 corner detail
1 Double glazing unit, vision glass area:
  outer lite of 8mm annealed glass; 12mm
  air-filled cavity; inner lite of 10mm two-ply
  laminated clear glass
2 Double glazing unit, shadow box area:
  outer lite of 8mm heat-strengthened glass;
  12mm air-filled cavity; inner lite of 8mm
  heat-strengthened glass
3 Double glazing unit, vision glass area:
  outer lite of 8mm toughened glass; 12mm
  air-filled cavity; inner lite of 10mm
  laminated clear glass
4 Double glazing unit: outer lite of 8mm green
  heat-strengthened glass with partial custom
  frit; 12mm air-filled cavity; inner lite of 10mm
  two-ply laminated low-e clear glass

J
Exterior corner detail of typical curtain wall
1 Double glazing unit, vision glass area
2 Local aluminum angle cleat in transoms to fix
  corner mullion
3 Painted aluminum extrusion, powder coat
4 Back of mullion
5 Horizontal mullion cap in projection below

K
Supergrid interior plan detail at levels 37–40

L
Supergrid plan detail at column location

M
Supergrid plan detail at typical wall
1 Double glazing unit, vision glass area
2 Structural column
3 Office column cover
4 1.2mm stainless steel bent sheet cover,
  brushed finish
5 1.2mm stainless steel, brushed finish
6 Insulation
7 Painted aluminum extrusion, powder coat
8 50mm diameter stainless steel rod,
  brushed finish

N
Plan detail of typical curtain wall
1 Double glazing unit, vision glass area: outer
  lite of 8mm annealed glass; 12mm air-filled
  cavity; inner lite of 10mm two-ply laminated
  clear glass
2 2.5mm stainless steel rod bracket
3 50mm diameter stainless steel rod,
  brushed finish
4 Painted aluminum extrusion, powder coat
5 1.5mm aluminum sheet, mill finish
6 Stainless steel angle cleat
7 Rigid insulation
8 1.2mm stainless steel sheet cover
9 Horizontal mullion cap in projection below
10 1.2mm stainless steel bent sheet cover
11 0.5mm stainless steel sheet, brushed finish

O
Section detail at typical curtain wall
1 Double glazing unit, vision glass area
2 Double glazing unit, shadow box area
3 Curtain wall anchor
4 Watertight seal every five floors
5 Firesmoke stop
6 3mm painted aluminum sheet, powder coat
7 Insulation
8 1.5mm backing steel sheet
9 Painted aluminum extrusion, powder coat
10 1.2mm bent stainless steel sheet, linen finish
11 Office ceiling
12 Office floor
13 0.5mm steel sheet
14 Concrete slab

Curtain wall visual and performance mock-up

Location
London, England
Dates
1999–2001
Client
Canary Wharf Contractors Limited
Building Program
Offices
Height
200 meters; 42 floors
Building Structural System
Concrete core with steel superstructure
Curtain Wall Type
Unitized
Mullions
Aluminum
Sunshades
Stainless steel with fine brushed finish
Spandrel Panel
Shadow box
Glass Type
**Sealed double glazing unit with high
performance coating**

Curtain Wall Manufacturer
Permasteelisa
CP&A Project Team
Design Principal: **Cesar Pelli**
Collaborating Designer and Project Principal:
Fred Clarke
Design Team Leader: **Lawrence Ng**
Designers: **Michael Hilgeman, Michael Cook,
Tomao Delgado**
Associate Architect
Adamson Associates
Structural Engineer
Yolles Partnership
Curtain Wall Consultant
Adamson Associates

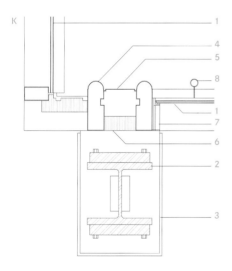

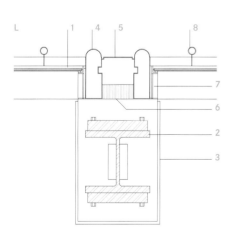

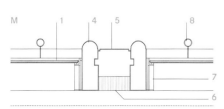

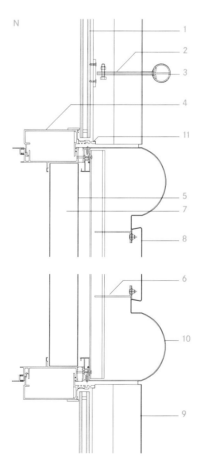

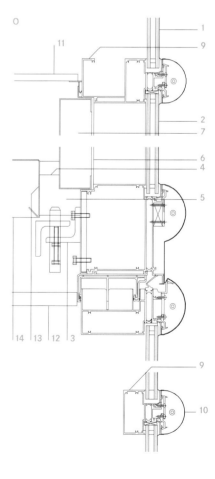

METAL

ONE CANADA SQUARE
LONDON

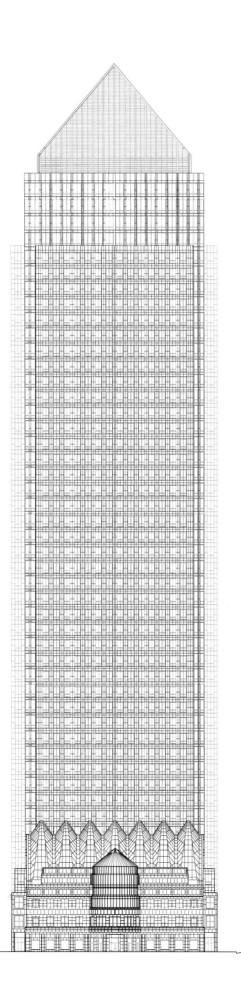

A

A
West elevation, scale 1:1000

B
Site plan

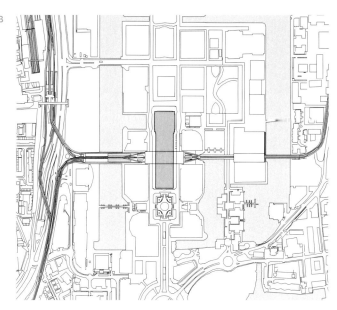

Context and Site: One Canada Square is the initial building in the large Canary Wharf corporate office development on approximately 28 hectares in the reclaimed Docklands section of London, and is considered the city's first skyscraper. A light rail system services the building — in fact the tower has its own stop on the rail line.

Architectural Form and Expression: Traditionally, London has been distinguished by figural buildings with pure architectural forms — such creations as St. Paul's Cathedral and the Houses of Parliament — meant as iconic symbols on the skyline. Canary Wharf Tower continues this tradition by adopting a similarly clear, strong, and powerful form.

At 236 meters in 48 stories, the building is a tall square prism with indented corners that culminate in a square pyramid against the sky. As England's first true skyscraper, Canary Wharf Tower appears to gleam softly in the gray and misty London atmosphere. The tower's corners are indented to reduce its apparent girth and to emphasize its height. This is accentuated by the inner tower core, which emerges from behind the outer walls and has larger windows that appear to balance the ratio of open to opaque curtain wall surface. The tower's articulated corners also welcome natural light to the interior, which reaches the inner ring of corridors on every floor.

Curtain Wall Components: The tower's exterior walls and pyramidal roof are clad with Type 316 stainless steel, which is dramatically expressive in the way it reflects changes in the sky's light and color. This grade of stainless steel has a higher percentage of nickel and molybdenum, compared to the more commonly used Type 304 material, which makes it more resistant to airborne sulfur and chlorides. British Steel and CP&A collaborated on the development of a finish called

HyClad Cambric, which has a more consistent surface appearance than the industry standard linen finish. The stainless steel has a cold-rolled finish with an embossed pattern, imprinted when the metal coil is fed through a series of rollers where the surfaces are ground, washed, annealed, stretched, embossed, and polished.

After milling, the direction in which the coil was fed into the rollers is marked with an arrow on the back of each panel. To ensure a uniform exterior, the 2.5mm-thick panels are all hung in the same orientation (arrows pointing up). Installing a panel in the reverse direction causes it to reflect light differently. To ensure their flatness, the panels are stiffened with channels welded to their back sides, along with anchors at the panel top. The stainless steel panels are then hung from the curtain wall's aluminum frame not unlike pictures on a wall, and tacked into place along their bottom edge. This allows them to expand and contract freely with temperature changes, and prevents the panels from bowing or "pillowing." Stainless steel ribs on the façade, articulated as thin double ribs vertically and a single rib horizontally, create a thin tracery of highlights that reflect the sunlight and subtly emphasize the tower's height. The glass is tinted with a soft champagne color and mounted in dark-painted aluminum frames — the overall effect of which is to reinforce the façade's appearance as a punched opening curtain wall.

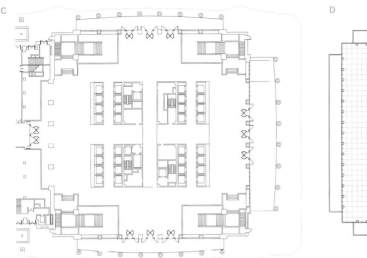

C

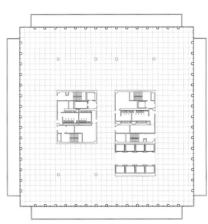

D

One Canada Square upon completion

West view of One Canada Square from
Canary Wharf

East view of One Canada Square from
Canary Wharf

Interior view of West Wintergarten

E

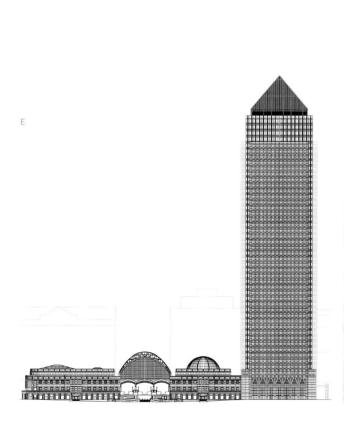

F
Section detail
1 300cm o.c. stainless steel studs
2 22 gauge galvanized steel air/vapor barrier
3 Frame expansion joint
4 Horizontal stiffner
5 2.5mm stainless steel panel
6 Rigid insulation

Detail view of corner setback

Curtain wall under construction

Curtain wall visual and performance mock-up

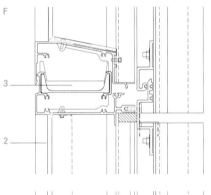

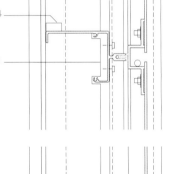

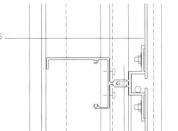

G
Typical plan detail
1 Aluminum plate 31.8 x 19mm, 3.2mm thick,
  inside horizontal moulding
2 2.3mm stainless steel panel type 316
3 44.5 x 44.5mm, 3.2mm thick aluminum plate
4 Neoprene corner plug over vision glass
  and panel
5 Rigid insulation

H
Typical plan detail
1 Aluminum mullion
2 3mm aluminum section
3 1.6mm roll formed stainless steel
  (big mosaic pattern)
4 Double glazing unit
5 22 gauge galvanized steel air/vapor barrier
6 Rigid insulation
7 22 gauge galvanized insulation strut
8 Interior sill trim
9 Window washing track

I
Typical section detail
1 Frame expansion joint
2 Neoprene corner plug
3 2.5mm stainless steel panel
  (big mosaic pattern)
4 Santoprene airseal gasket
5 Set block
6 Pressure equalizing clots, two per cap
7 Santoprene glazing gasket
8 Steel T 100 x 100 x 75mm, 6.4mm thick
9 22 gauge galvanized steel bracket
10 Double glazing unit
11 Rigid insulation

Location
London, England
Dates
1986–1991
Client
Olympia & York
Building Program
Offices
Height
236 meters; 48 floors
Building Structural System
All steel structure
Curtain Wall Type
Unitized
Mullions
Aluminum
Spandrel Panels
Stainless steel
Glass Type
Sealed double glazing unit with low-e coating
Curtain Wall Manufacturer
Permasteelisa

CP&A Project Team
Design Principal: Cesar Pelli
Collaborating Designer and Project Principal:
Fred Clarke
Project Managers: Thomas Morton, Jeff Paine
Design Team Leaders: Robert Bostwick,
Lawrence Ng, Robert Taylor, Lisa Winkelmann
Designers: David Chen, David Johnson, Dewitt
Zuac, Sarah Amolar, John Apicella, Ruth Bennett,
Sunny Evangelista Carroll, Michael Green,
Jong-Gon Kim, Maki Kuwayama, Julia Parker,
Michael Petti, Matthias Richter, Frank Sheng,
David Scklar, Bret Sleeper, Bettina Stark,
Roberta Weinberg, Masami Yonezawa
Associate Architect
Adamson Associates
Structural Engineer
W.S. Atkins Transportation Engineering,
Epsom, Surrey; M.S. Yolles & Partners, Toronto;
M.S. Yolles & Partners Ltd., London
Curtain Wall Consultant
Israel Berger & Associates

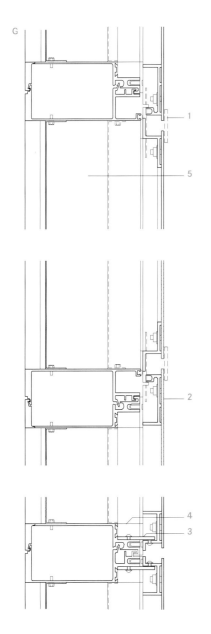

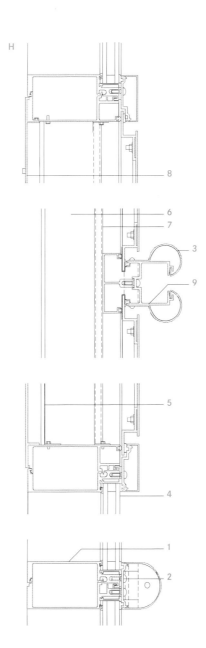

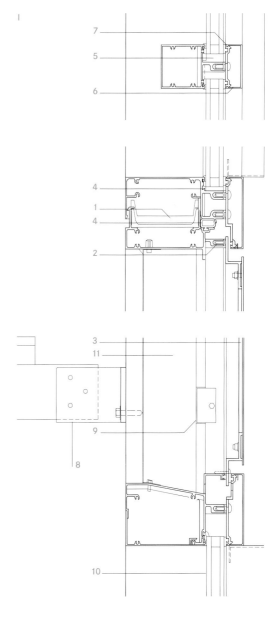

JP MORGAN CHASE
SAN FRANCISCO

A

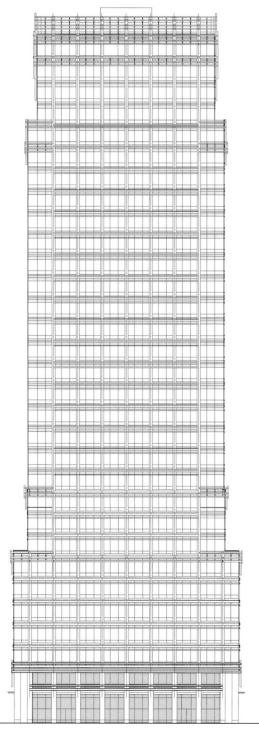

A
Mission Street elevation, scale 1:1000

B
Site plan

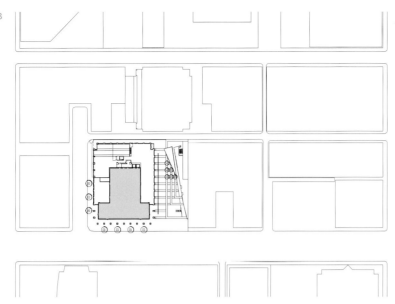

Context and Site: This $200 million development is located in downtown San Francisco, in the north-east corner of the city, not far from the Bay Bridge. The developer of this project, Hines, was interested in stretching the city's esthetic guidelines, which over the years have resulted in a preponderance of new buildings rendered in light-colored limestone. The clients and the architect surveyed other buildings in the city's architectural context such as the Hallidie Building of 1918, one of the first suspended glass curtain wall structures in the U.S. and just a few blocks north-west of Mission Street, which served as the inspiration for the building's design.

The project includes a 1300-square-meter plaza and urban park, complete with a bamboo grove and an 84-square-meter stone fountain.

Architectural Form and Expression: The design of JP Morgan Chase is both modern and classical. The building's form as a stately tower that rises in a series of setbacks is in keeping with its dense urban fabric. The composition is classical in its symmetrical arrangement, while the glass walls suggest an uncompromisingly modern structure. The Hallidie Building's large glass openings are suggested in JP Morgan Chase's ample, horizontal fenestration pattern. This also recognized the client's wish that the building's interiors be light and airy, with the sense of being suspended in mid-air.

Curtain Wall Components: Recalling the Hallidie Building's use of steel and cast iron to describe an ornate façade, JP Morgan Chase uses a weave of aluminum channels to provide surface richness. The building's structure is on a 10-meter module, which results in generous window bays that lend the façade a horizontal emphasis. The bays are further divided into tripartite panels, suggesting Chicago windows.

The articulation of the tower's surface is achieved through a sophisticated weaving of vertical and horizontal aluminum channels (a different language than the sleek bullnoses and rounded shapes found on many of Pelli's curtain walls). The richest texture is within the first block of the building, and becomes increasingly fine and spare as the tower ascends and steps back. However, the final setback explodes in a restoration of the texture, which crowns the tower with a cornice-like study in shade and shadow.

The interlaced aluminum sections start with strong vertical members, which are then overlaid by three horizontal strands, and then another strong vertical channel. At certain levels in the curtain wall a belt of horizontal channels encircles the building, suggesting a decorative band. At the tower's four corners the weave becomes flatter and less three-dimensional, and the glazing more flush with the mullions. From a distance the corners read as modern versions of quoins.

The color selected for the painted aluminum is a very dark glossy green (approaching black), which is consistent throughout the curtain wall. This high-performance coating is complementary to the glass, and the high-gloss finish provides enough contrast so that the edges of the channels read as crisp threads in the weave.

Insulated glass is used for both the vision and spandrel panels. The glazing has a low-e coating on number 2 surface, with no tinting or reflective coating. The spandrel glass has a dark gray paint coating to the number 4 surface, which gives the material an appearance similar to that of the vision panel.

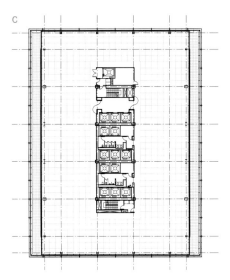

East view of Mission Street and plaza elevations

Tower top crown

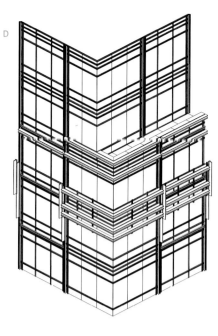

West elevation along Mission Street

E
Typical wall axonometric
General note: all wall elements are extruded aluminum painted with a durable two-coat system. Color is a custom deep, lush green

1 Horizontal mullion at floor slab with interior slab edge closure panel
2 Horizontal mullion at 0.61m sill line, unitized panel stack joint location with internal guttering and air seal
3 Horizontal mullion at ceiling line
4 False horizontal trim: surface applied to spandrel glass with silicone sealant
5 Floating horizontal accent: floats in front of floating vertical accents, attached mechanically to side of primary vertical accent
6 Primary vertical mullion with accent: vertical mullion with unitized panel joint and mechanically attached exterior accent trim
7 Floating vertical accent: exterior trim on either side of primary vertical, mechanically attached to face of horizontal mullion
8 Secondary vertical mullion with minimal exterior "snap on" trim and unitized joints
9 Vision glass: clear insulated unit with high performance low-e coating, tempered unit
10 Vision glass: below stack joint, clear insulated unit with low-e coating, tempered unit
11 Spandrel glass: clear insulated unit with low-e coating and a custom color ceramic frit floodcoat opacifier on #4 surface

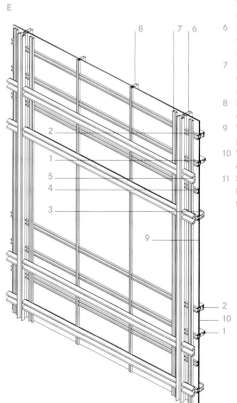

Curtain wall under construction

Curtain wall performance mock-up

View of plaza level colonnade

Detail view of 8th floor corner setback

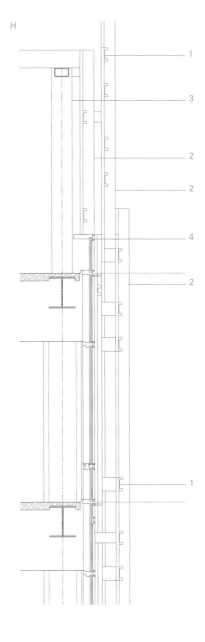

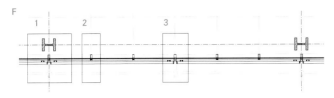

F

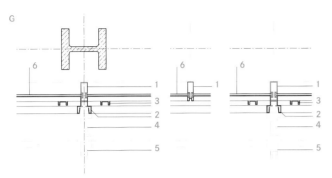

G

Location
San Francisco, California
Dates
1998–2002
Client
**HInes with the National Office Partners
Limited Partnership**
Building Program
Offices
Height
142 meters; 31 floors
Building Structural System
Steel structure
Curtain Wall Type
Unitized panel system
Mullions
**Painted aluminum extrusions and
breakform panels**
Sunshades
**Painted aluminum extrusions and
breakform panels**
Spandrel Panels
Clear insulated glass, low-e coating and

a ceramic frit floorcoat on #4 surface
Glass Type
Clear insulated glass with low-e coating
Lighting
**Vertical accent uplights at upper setback and
roof level**
Curtain Wall Manufacturer
**Enclos (Design, coordination and installation)
Baker Metal Products (Design and fabrication)**
CP&A Project Team
**Design Principal: Cesar Pelli
Collaborating Designer and Project Principal:
Fred Clarke
Design Team Leaders: Anthony Markese,
Edward Dionne
Designers: Projjal Dutta, John Apicella,
Barbara Endres**
Associate Architect
Kendall/Heaton Associates
Structural Engineer
CBM Engineers
Curtain Wall Consultant
Peter Muller

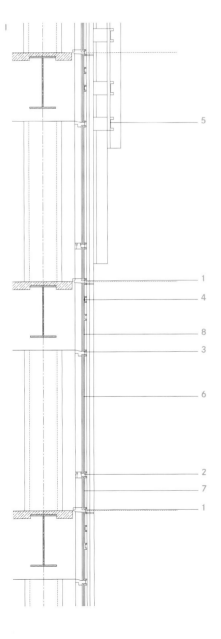

I

F
Plan of typical structural bay
1 Vertical mullion: functional unitized mullion
   system with internal gutter and centered
   unit panel joint
2 Primary vertical accent trim: "snap on"
   accent trim, interlocking with functional
   mullion
3 Floating vertical accent: exterior trim on
   either side of primary vertical, mechanically
   attached to face of horizontal mullion

G
Typical plan details
1 Vertical mullion: functional unitized mullion
   system with internal gutter and centered
   unit panel joint
2 Primary vertical accent trim: "snap on"
   accent trim, interlocking with functional
   mullion
3 Floating vertical accent: exterior trim on
   either side of primary vertical, mechanically
   attached to face of horizontal mullions
4 Vertical accent trim #1: setback and
   tower top only. Mechanically attached to
   primary vertical
5 Vertical accent trim #2: setbacks and
   tower top only
6 Vision glass: clear, insulated unit with high
   performance low-e coating

H
Wall section detail at tower top crown
1 Floating horizontal accent: attached by
   bracket arm to primary verticals
2 Vertical accent trim, mechanically attached
   to primary verticals
3 Structural support for crown accents: painted
   steel, custom color to match exterior wall
4 Parapet cap: painted aluminum

I
Wall section detail on upper floors
1 Horizontal mullion at floor slab with interior
   slab edge closure panel
2 Horizontal mullion at 0.61m sill line,
   unitized panel stack joint location with
   internal guttering and airseal
3 Horizontal mullion at ceiling line
4 False horizontal trim: surface applied to
   spandrel glass with silicone sealant
5 Floating horizontal accent: attached by
   bracket arm to primary verticals (setbacks
   and tower top only)
6 Vision glass: clear, insulated unit with high
   performance low-e coating
7 Vision glass: below stack joint, clear insulated unit with low-e coating, tempered unit
8 Spandrel glass: clear insulated unit with
   low-e coating and a custom color ceramic frit
   floodcoat opacifier on surface #4

731 LEXINGTON AVENUE
NEW YORK

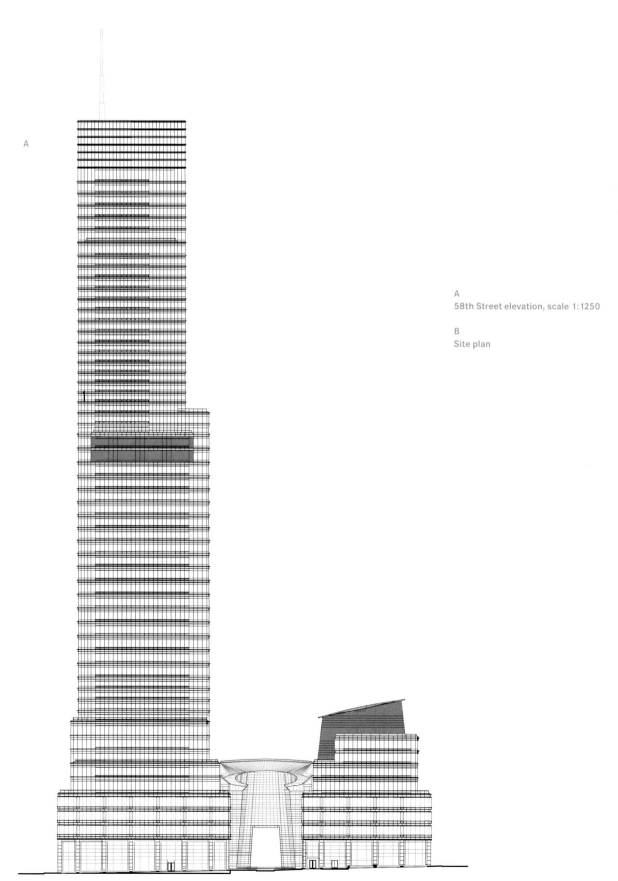

A

A
58th Street elevation, scale 1:1250

B
Site plan

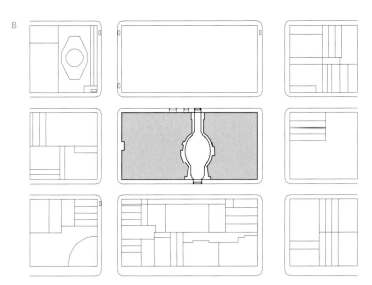

Context and Site: This 55-story tower is located on a full-block site between Lexington and Third Avenues and 58th and 59th Streets. It is a pivotal site on the edge of the Midtown and East Side residential districts along the Lexington Avenue retail corridor, uniquely suited to a mix of residential, commercial, and retail uses.

The tower has extensive views of Central Park and contains both office space and a mix of luxury condominiums. The tower is also the new signature headquarters for the financial and media giant Bloomberg, housing nearly 4000 of its employees.

Architectural Form and Expression: The 248-meter tower is an elegant crystalline form against the sky. The base of the building features a mid-block exterior public space known as Beacon Court that allows multiple formal entries with canopies and vehicular drop-off. This space carved out of the seven-story base is elliptical in plan and conical in shape. Initially created to reconcile conflicting programmatic and traffic concerns the courtyard has evolved into a dramatic signature public space rarely seen in New York. The Lexington Avenue office lobby features high ceilings and a generous use of stone and fine woods to create a space of distinction commensurate with the quality exhibited throughout the project. Capped by a softly glowing crown, One Beacon Court exemplifies its name — a luminous, new beacon on the skyline of Manhattan.

Curtain Wall Components: One of the design goals of this mixed-use building was to give the curtain wall a consistent appearance for both office and residential spaces. For this reason, the curtain wall design is flexible enough to work for both uses. The wall's strong horizontal emphasis accommodates residential spaces (including operable windows) and also allows a maximum of light and views for the office spaces.

The tower is layered principally with glassy floors, between which are expressive bullnose moldings executed in painted aluminum (which serve to hide the spandrel portion of the curtain wall). A variety of colors was studied to determine how they would appear in different kinds of light and how they fit with the context. The beige color was chosen because it communicates the message that this is primarily a residential tower (it was felt that a material such as stainless steel would be too institutional in appearance). The classically composed bullnoses also seem appropriate for a residential structure and suggest the context of fine, older New York apartment buildings from the turn of the last century. The top surface of the bullnose slants away from the building at 30 degrees to prevent pigeons from roosting and to repel ice and snow.

The tower's glass is a delicate balance between transparency and solidity. It has enough reflectivity to hold the tower on the skyline, and sufficient transparency to allow views into the building. The double-pane insulated glass is clear, with no applied tinting.

The podium and courtyard curtain wall has a different treatment altogether. Here the dominant material is naturally finished stainless steel, which lends a bit more formality to the building in the public space of the through-block courtyard. This structurally glazed curtain wall is supported by an external stainless steel tube and rod system.

C
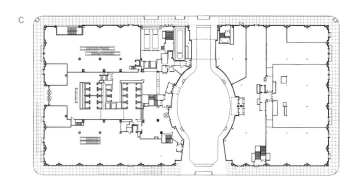

D
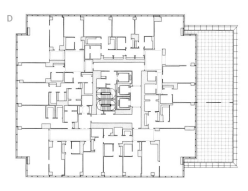

East elevation from Beacon Court

C
Ground floor plan

D
Floor plan level 32, residential

Beacon Court curtain wall visual and
performance mock-up

E

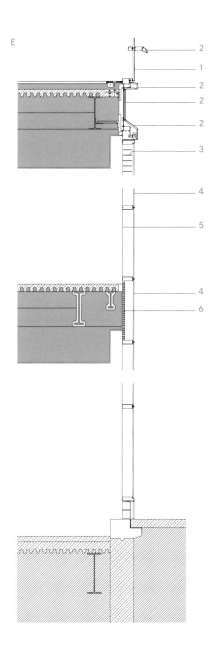

F

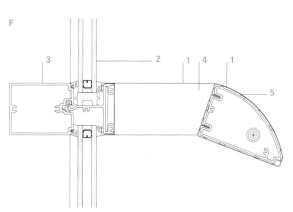

G

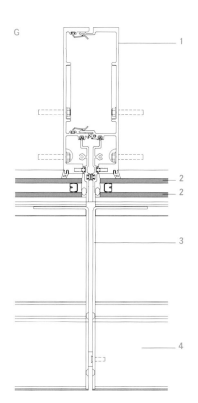

E
Section of storefront façade
1 Insulated glass
2 Stainless steel #4
3 Stainless steel grill
4 19mm glass
5 Stainless steel #4
6 Shadow box

F
Section of podium curtain wall, mullion detail
1 Stainless steel #4 bar
2 Insulated glass
3 Painted metal
4 Stainless steel #4 bracket
5 Stainless steel #4 rail

G
Plan detail of vertical mullion/podium
1 Vertical mullion, painted metal
2 Insulated glass unit
3 Stainless steel #4 bracket
4 Stainless steel #4 rail

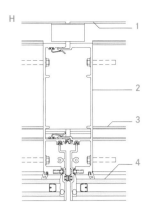
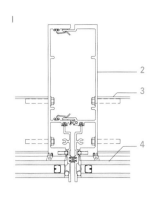
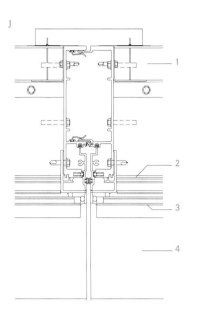

H
Plan detail of vertical mullion at sill (tower)
1 Painted metal sill trim below
2 Painted metal
3 Line of horizontal mullion
4 Insulated glass

I
Plan detail of vertical mullion at typical
horizontal member (tower)

J
Plan detail of vertical mullion at typical
spandrel panel (tower)
1 Insulation
2 Line of seal
3 Painted metal spandrel panel
4 Stainless steel spandrel panel below

East elevation from street level with
Queensboro bridge and Roosevelt Island Tram

Detail view of lower level office curtain wall

Tower curtain wall mock-up

Beacon Court curtain wall visual and
performance mock-up

K
Section of tower curtain wall, mullion detail
1 Painted metal
2 Insulated glass

L
Section of podium at setback

K

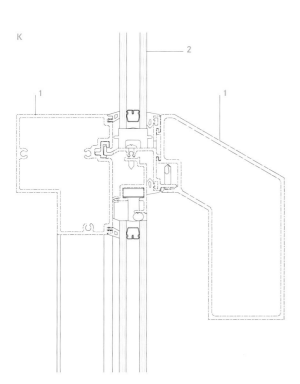

L

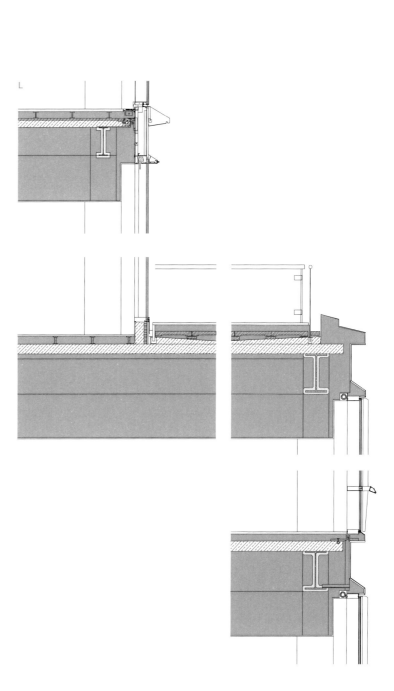

Detail view of lower office level curtain wall

View of east elevation from Beacon Court

M

Section detail at podium floors 3–5
1 Fin tube
2 Raised floor
3 Stainless steel #4
4 Insulated glass
5 Painted aluminum

N
Section detail at tower floors 6 and above

O
Section at Beacon Court

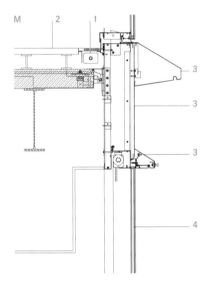

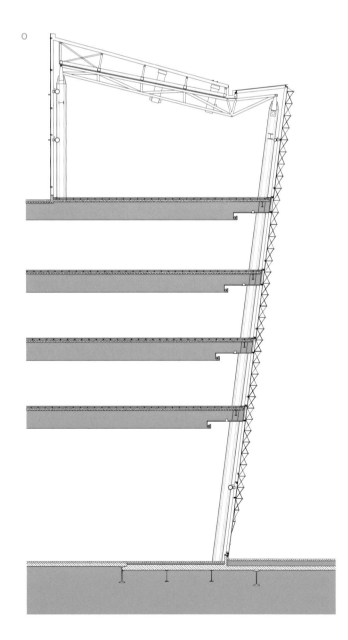

Location
New York, New York
Dates
1999–2005
Client
Vornado Realty Trust
Building Program
Mixed use
Height
248 meters; 51 floors
Building Structural System
Steel up to 29th floor; 29th floor is a hybrid of steel and concrete; floors 30 and above concrete
Curtain Wall Type
Storefront: modified unitized system with oversized elements (8.2 x 3 meters) with "lightning bolt" corners coming to site as single unit
Beacon Court: hybrid cassette system
Podium and tower: unitized system
Mullions
Storefront: stainless steel #4 finish with both tempered clear glass and opaque laminated glass

Beacon Court: stainless steel
Interior mullions: painted aluminum
Insulated glass at second floor and above: clear glass with low-e coating on #2 surface
Shadow box panels: clear glass with low-e coating on #2 surface with painted metal back panel
Glass Type
First floor: laminated reeded glass, laminated translucent glass and low-iron glass
Podium: insulated glass
Tower: insulated glass
Shadow box panels: low-e glass with painted metal back panel
Tower lantern: laminated glass, clear glass with white, translucent interlayer
Lighting
Tower lantern: cold cathode tubes mounted to back of curtain wall and project onto a white wall 91cm away. The cold cathode tubes are dimmable and change from warm white to cold white as the evening progresses

Curtain Wall Manufacturer
Enclos; Baker Metal Products
CP&A Project Team
Design Principal: Cesar Pelli
Collaborating Designer and Project Principal: Rafael Pelli
Design Team Leaders: Mark Shoemaker, Robyn Sandberg
Designers: Karin Patriquin, Taek Park, Mamta Prakash-Dutta, William Greaves, Michael Harshman, Ulises Liceaga, Florencia Moralejo, Gregorio Santamaria, Derk Scholtz
Associate Architect
SLCE
Structural Engineer
Thornton-Tomasetti Engineers
Curtain Wall Consultant
Israel Berger & Associates

P

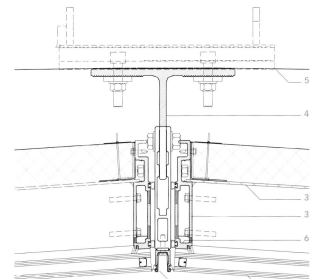

Q

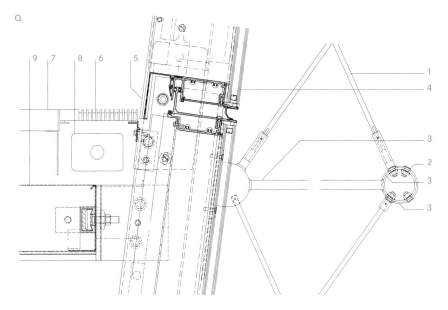

P

Plan of Beacon Court curtain wall/slab connection
1 Stainless steel #4 fins
2 Vision glass, insulated
3 Painted metal
4 T-anchor
5 Slab edge
6 Structural silicone
7 Stainless steel accent bar

Q

Section of Beacon Court curtain wall, stack joint detail
1 Stainless steel #4 rod
2 Stainless steel #4 continuously curved tube
3 Stainless steel #4 support system
4 Insulated glass
5 Painted metal
6 Floor register
7 Raised floor
8 Fin tube
9 Concrete slab

EDIFICIO REPÚBLICA
BUENOS AIRES

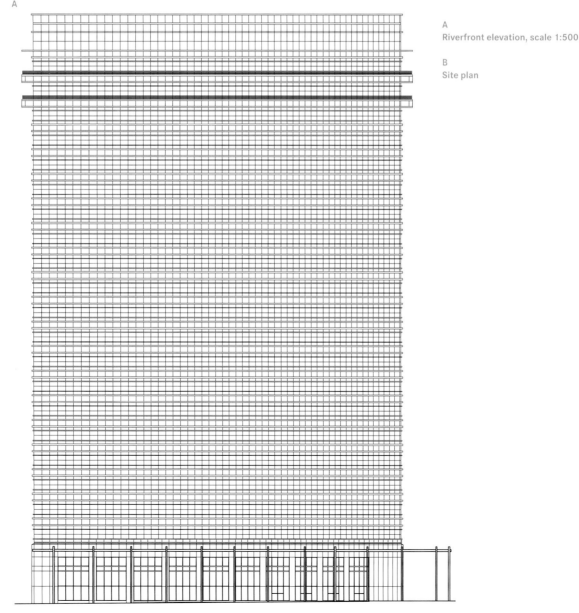

A
Riverfront elevation, scale 1:500

B
Site plan

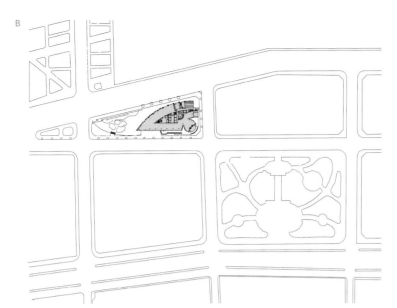

Context and Site: The 23,000-square-meter Edificio República office building adapts itself to a triangular block between Bouchard Street, Madero, Tucumán, and Viamonte streets. This site at the border of the city features a building with a broad convex curve with views towards Madero and the Rio de la Plata. The building offers views of the river on one side and to the city on the other. The corner facing Plaza Roma has a large concave "ochava" (a chamfer at the building's corner edge). It recognizes this important public place and salutes it.

Architectural Form and Expression: A large curved wall opens to the sweeping view of the river. On the building's obverse side, the urban importance of the corner is accentuated by a five-story cylindrical volume with a terrace garden and a main entrance that faces Plaza Roma. The façades pointing toward the city conform to vertical planes that define the street space, while a celebratory concave corner faces Plaza Roma. On the upper floors, two continuous balconies make reference to the traditional architecture of Buenos Aires, whereas the solid base resembles the old arcades of Alem Avenue. On the ground level, a winter garden and an assembly hall can be used together or separately for conferences, concerts, banquets, and exhibitions. The winter garden opens toward a public plaza, and a metal-and-glass canopy defines a transition space.

Curtain Wall Components: The 90-meter-tall building is clad in a painted aluminum curtain wall that furthers the project's larger design goals. The curtain wall's design reinforces the shape of the building with its sweeping horizontal emphasis. Each floor level is punctuated by three bands of aluminum tubes (one below and one above the spandrel panel, with a smaller-diameter band just above the vision panel), held aloft from the building's face. The primary function of the large

and small tubular bands (approximately 200mm and 100mm in diameter, respectively) is to create horizontal shadow lines that give the curtain wall added depth.

The white banding suggests the stone detailing on Buenos Aires' older buildings. Varieties of white shades were studied. The final color is a warm tone with a flat finish, making another visual connection with the city's tradition of masonry architecture, often rendered in light colors.

Three types of glass give the curtain wall a multiplicity of subtle readings. The insulated vision glass has a slight reflective coating that allows relatively clear views out of and into the building. The spandrel panel glass is more reflective to provide a sharper horizontal emphasis. Above the vision panel is a transom panel, identical in height to the spandrel glass. The transom glass has the same reflectivity as the vision glass, but with a ceramic frit pattern applied to the number 2 surface. The 3mm-diameter polka dot frit lends a texture to the glass that gives the curtain wall an added dimension and once again reinforces the building's horizontal expression.

C

D

C
Ground floor plan

D
First floor plan

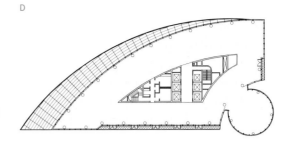

Night view towards Río De La Plata

View towards Río De La Plata

Detail view of corner drum

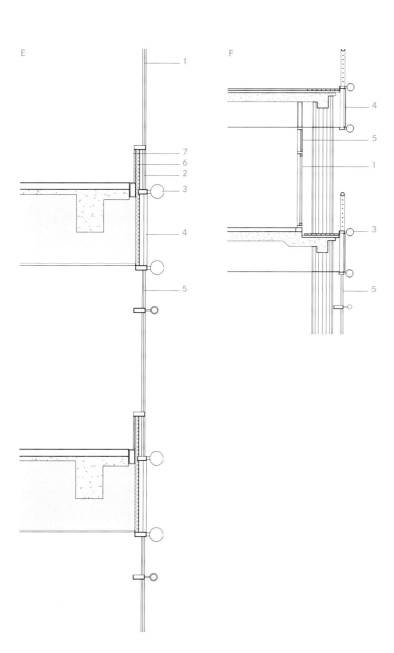

E
Typical wall section

F
Section through corner drum
1 Typical vision glass: 25.4mm insulated units
   with 6mm reflective coating on #2 surface,
   13mm airspace, 6mm clear glass
2 Typical spandrel glass: 6mm reflective glass
   with polyester opacifier on #2 surface
3 Horizontal accent aluminum tube: 200mm
   diameter, 4mm wall, two-coat paint system
   with flash primer
4 Metal panel: 3mm aluminum with stiffeners,
   two-coat paint system with flash primer
5 Typical transom glass: 25.4mm insulated
   units with reflective glass with silkscreen,
   6mm glass with ceramic frit on #2 surface,
   13mm airspace, 6mm clear glass
6 64mm insulation
7 Gypsum plasterboard

G
Typical plan detail of transom lite
1 Vertical mullion: painted aluminum, two-coat system with flash primer
2 Typical transom glass: 25.4mm insulated units with reflective glass and silkscreen, 6mm glass with ceramic frit on #2 surface, 13mm airspace, 6mm clear glass
3 Horizontal accent aluminum tube: 100mm diameter, 3mm wall, two-coat system with flash primer
4 Transom glass frame: painted aluminum, two-coat system with flash primer
5 Projection of miniblind
6 Tube end caps

Curtain wall performance mock-up

Curtain wall performance mock-up

Detail view of curtain wall corner

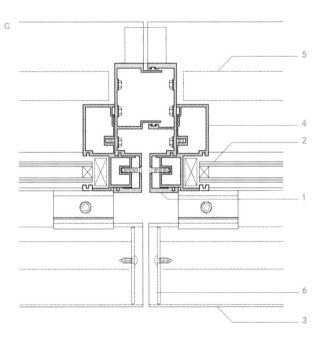

H
Typical wall section detail
7   Gypsum plasterboard
8   Anchor, chromate
9   Concrete floor slab
10 Typical transom glass: 25.4mm insulated
    units with reflective glass and silkscreen,
    6mm glass with ceramic frit on #2 surface,
    13mm airspace, 6mm clear glass
11 Spandrel glass: 6mm reflective glass with
    polyester opacifier on #2 surface

I
Typical wall section detail
12 Miniblind
13 64mm thermal insulation
14 Metal panel: 3mm aluminum with stiffeners,
    two-coat paint system with flash primer

Location
Buenos Aires, Argentina
Dates
1992 – 1996
Client
República Propiedades, SA
Building Program
Offices
Height
90 meters; 21 floors (including mechanical floor)
Building Structural System
Poured-in-place reinforced concrete
Curtain Wall Type
Unitized
Mullions
Painted aluminum
Sunshades
Painted aluminum tubes
Spandrel Panels
Painted aluminum panels
Glass Type
Vision: reflective glass
Spandrel: reflective glass with polyester

opacifier
**Transom windows: reflective glass with
ceramic frit pattern**
Storefront: laminated clear glass
Lighting
Fiber optics at balcony levels
Curtain Wall Manufacturer
Benson Industries
CP&A Project Team
Design Principal: Cesar Pelli
**Collaborating Designer and Project Principal:
Fred Clarke**
**Project Manager: Philip Bernstein,
Susana La Porta Drago**
Design Team Leader: Robert Bostwick
Designers: Heather Young, Alberto Zan
Associate Architect
**Mario Roberto Alvarez y Asociados,
Buenos Aires**
Structural Engineer
Alberto Fainstein y Asociados SA, Buenos Aires
Curtain Wall Consultant
Peter M. Muller

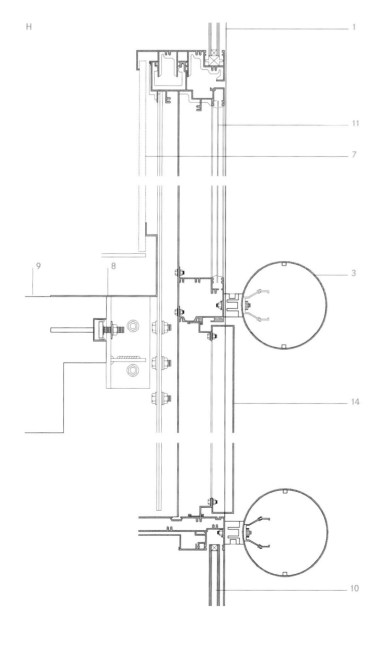

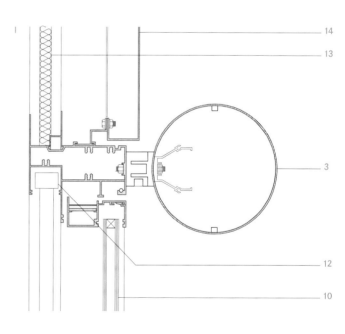

MORI OFFICE TOWER
TOKYO

A

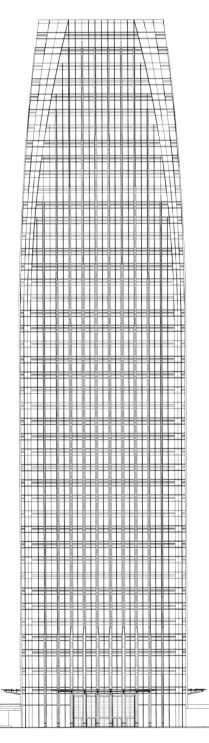

A
East elevation, scale 1:1000

B
Site plan

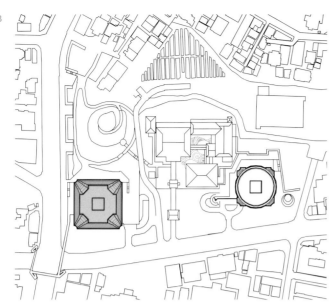

Context and Site: The Mori Office Tower is part of the Atago Green Hills development, comprising a modern array of offices, residences, and shops adjacent to Mt. Atago and the Seisho-ji Temple. Surrounded by Atago-yama and Shiba Parks, the Atago area offers year-round access to lush verdant parks. Situated between two major business districts and adjacent to many hotels and embassies, the Atago area is developing into a first-grade business center of Tokyo.

Commissioned by the Mori Corporation, the project combines the redesign of a large public park with the integration of an existing Zen Buddhist Temple and two 42-story towers – the Mori Office Tower and the Forest Residential Tower.

Architectural Form and Expression: The form of the Mori Office Tower is in the spirit of its sister building, the Forest Residential Tower, and is quite unique in its sculptural expression. The Office Tower begins at its base as a square-shaped monolith whose chamfered edges splay wider as the building rises, resulting in a gently tapered form. In addition to the splayed corner chamfers, the four principal façades of the building gently slope back as the tower reaches its peak. The effect is not unlike the opening of the petals of a lotus blossom, which is an appropriate organic reference in this context. This sophisticated approach to form-making works well with the client's wish to maximize the rentable floor space.

The structure of both the office and the residential towers feature advance seismic design. The buildings are configured to safely withstand an earthquake of 7.0 on the Richter scale. This results in far greater levels of comfort and safety for building occupants as well as enhanced security of operations than typically available in other Tokyo office and residential buildings.

Curtain Wall Components: The Mori Office Tower is clad with a dramatically shaped, vertically organized metal curtain wall with a sculptural columnar emphasis. The building's perimeter tube structure is expressed through the vertical emphasis of the curtain wall, with its bent, painted aluminum tubular elements, 4mm thick, that race up the façade, catching the light as they go. While rising, the columns become smaller and smaller (accentuating the building's height) and their cylindrical reading begins to diminish. At sidewalk level the building has a strong topographic rhythm of columns. As the curtain wall ascends it becomes tauter — a faithful expression of the tower's tapering form.

The reflective glass helps to convey the tower's slick surface, emphasizing its overall form. The same material is used for both the vision and the spandrel glass. A white ceramic frit pattern is found on the spandrel panel glass, starting as a fairly dense finish that becomes thinner at the tower top. There are ten frit densities in all, and their effect is to make the tower appear more solid as it meets the ground and to make it dissipate and be more reflective and glassy as it reaches the sky. In the same way, the graphic interweaving of the horizontal and vertical elements is strongest and more three-dimensional at the base, and looser and more ethereal at the top.

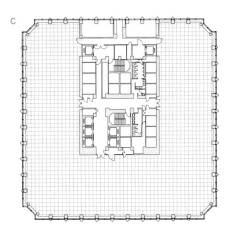
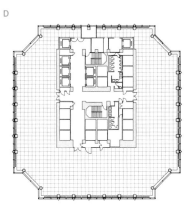

View from upper level office floor

Night view of south-east elevation

E

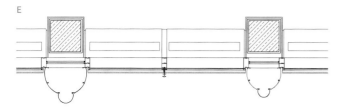

F

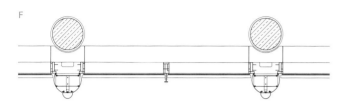

North elevation

G

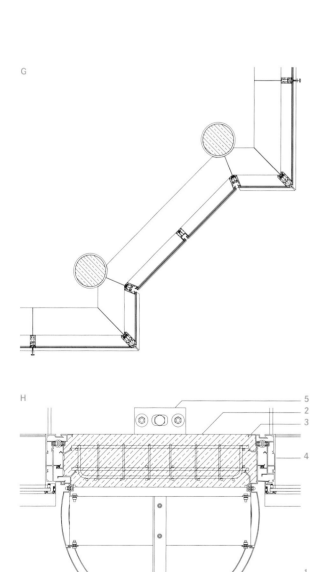

H

Detail view of canopy

Ground level view from north

Detail view of curtain wall reflecting the Forest Residential Tower

I

J

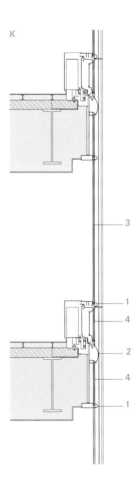

K

3

1
4

2

4

1

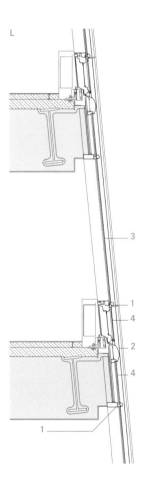

L

3

1
4

2

4

1

Tower top under construction

Location	Curtain Wall Manufacturer
Tokyo, Japan	**Shin nikkei Co. Ltd.**
Dates	CP&A Project Team
1995–2002	**Design Principal: Cesar Pelli**
Client	**Collaborating Designer and Project Principal:**
Mori Corporation	**Fred Clarke**
Building Program	**Design Team Leader: Gregg Jones**
Offices	**Designers: Takahiro Sato, Pablo Lopez, Natasha**
Hcight	**Boyd, Projjal Dutta, Keith Krolak, Martina Lind,**
186.75 meters; 42 floors	**Marcella Staudenmaier**
Building Structural System	Associate Architect
Steel frame with concrete-filled columns	**Cesar Pelli & Associates Japan Inc., Tokyo, Japan**
Curtain Wall Type	Curtain Wall Consultant
Unitized	**Peter M. Muller/Benson Industries**
Mullions	
Fluoropolymer-coated aluminum	
Spandrel Panels	
Ceramic frit glass and boards, hard-anodized aluminum fins	
Glass Type	
Vision: heat-strengthened reflective glass	
Spandrel: heat-strengthened reflective glass with ceramic frit pattern	

I
Tower top section

J
Corner section

K
Curtain wall configurations, lower floor
1 Hard anodized extruded aluminum cap
2 Fluoropolymer-coated, extruded
  aluminum panel
3 High-performance reflective insulated
  vision glass
4 Frit-patterned spandrel glass

L
Curtain wall configurations, upper floor

M
Detail section at stack joint
1 Hard anodized extruded aluminum cap
2 Fluoropolymer-coated, extruded
  aluminum mullion
3 High-performance reflective insulated
  vision glass
4 Frit-patterned spandrel glass
5 Steel window sill

N
Detail section at fastener
1 Fluoropolymer-coated, extruded
  aluminum panel
2 Frit-patterned spandrel glas
3 Fluoropolymer-coated, extruded
  aluminum mullion
4 Fastener
5 Floor slab
6 Air intake slot

M

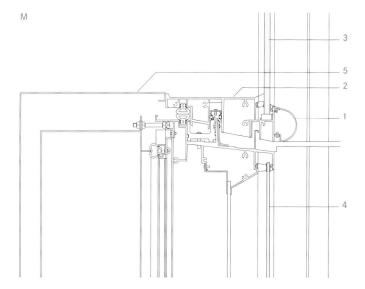

N

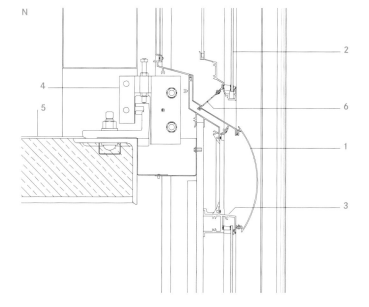

NTT HEADQUARTERS
TOKYO

A

A
East elevation, scale 1:750

B
Site plan

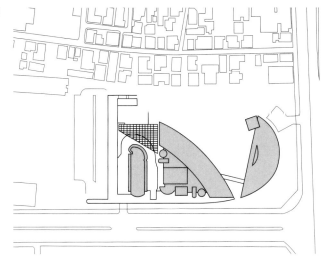

Context and Site: The NTT Headquarters – which includes a 30-story tower, a special-purpose building, and an open garden – is an extension of the cultural, corporate, and commercial center of Shinjuku. The site is six blocks away from the Tokyo City Hall and two blocks from the Opera House. The design responds to several limitations: there is an elevated highway to the south front of the site; over 20 percent of the site is dedicated to public open space; a maximum height of 127 meters for the tower was established by the city and the neighborhood; the building had to avoid two existing microwave corridors for communications and the roof had to accommodate transmission equipment and also emergency helicopter landing and its flight paths. Sunlight access regulations required that the building be shaped so that no single point of the neighboring residential properties was under shadow for more than three hours each day.

Architectural Form and Expression: The character, form, and composition of the tower, special-purpose building, and garden fit appropriately in the Shinjuku district. The fan-shaped tower of offices is oriented toward the interior garden and the long views; support facilities occupy the remainder of the allowable triangular envelope. The office portion of the tower is organized with horizontal windows to take advantage of the panoramic view. The tower is expressed as a curved form that responds to the various site constraints and opportunities. The special-purpose building has a tightly curved wall that opens to views of the interior garden. Its eastern side is anchored by a vertical volume with special function rooms. A wall screens a parking lot and an automobile entrance and drop off. Paved with loose gravel so that it can be used for exhibitions and performances, the garden has trees, a fountain, a wood bridge, and a fence of composite materials including wood and steel.

Curtain Wall Components: The office tower is glad with a painted aluminum curtain wall distinguished by sweeping horizontal windows that alternate with bands of metal spandrel panels. The windows are protected by four rows of projecting sunshades per floor. The sunshades accentuate the horizontality of the windows, modulate the façade, and animate it with shadows and highlights throughout the day. The aluminum components are coated with a metallic paint specially formulated for this building. The gray color is suggestive of the gunmetal tone that is commonly seen in Japanese tiles, rendered with more luster and sparkle. The silvery color reflects the variously changing blue, gray, and white colors of the sky. The size of the paint's metal flakes was carefully studied to achieve just the right reflectivity and color with a high density of flake.

The curtain wall's glass is clearly transparent (there is a very slight gray cast that complements the painted aluminum). The transparency renders outside colors truly when viewed from inside. The glass selected has some reflectivity thanks to a high-performance sputtered stainless steel coating, but it is not overt. The glass reflects roughly 20 percent of the sunlight that hits its surface.

The special-purpose building contains uses that do not require abundant natural light and views, so its curtain wall is highly opaque in contrast to the tower. This tightly curved wall of imported Minnesota stone on the street side opens to views of the interior garden. The wing's eastern side is clad in green Vermont slate.

C

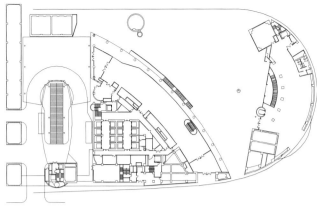

D

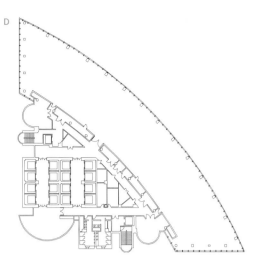

South-east elevation

Street level view from Yamanote Dori

Night view of courtyard

North-east elevation

E

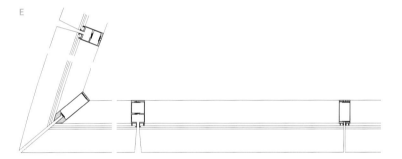

F

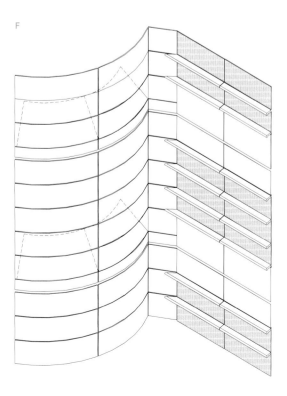

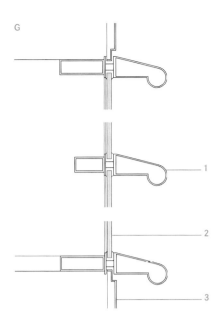

Sample curtain wall module

Tower under construction

Two details of tower curtain wall

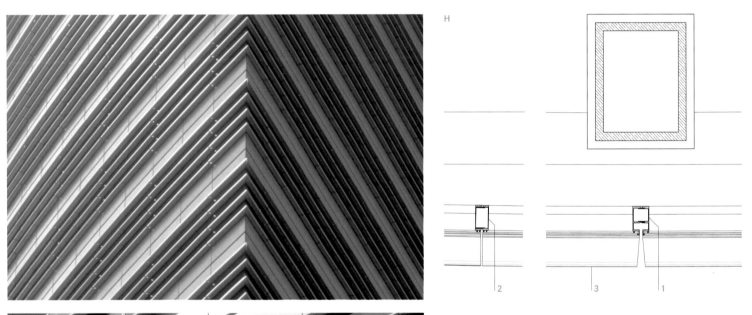

Detail of special-purpose building curtain wall

Location	Glass Type
Tokyo, Japan	**High-performance glass**
Dates	**(Heat reflecting glass)**
1990–1995	Curtain Wall Manufacturer
Client	**Tostem Corp & Kawneer; Nihon Kentetsu Co.,**
NTT Corporation	**Ltd. & Benson Ltd.; Nikkei Urban Build Co.**
Building Program	**Ltd. & Harmon**
Headquarters	CP&A Project Team
Height	**Design Principal: Cesar Pelli**
127 meters; 30 floors	**Collaborating Designer and Project Principal:**
Building Structural System	**Fred Clarke**
Concrete-encased steel	**Design Team Leaders: Jun Mitsui, Gregg Jones,**
Curtain Wall Type	**David Chen**
Unitized	**Designers: Scott Aquilina, Ruth Bennett, Kevin**
Mullions	**Burke, Roberto Espejo, Karen Koenig-Johnson,**
Extruded fluoropolymer-coated aluminum with	**Douglas McIntosh, Hirotaka Otsuji, Roger**
a metallic gray finish	**Schickedantz, Masami Yonasawa**
Sunshades	Associate Architect
Bent heavy gauge aluminum panels (in part)	**Yamashita Sekkei Inc., Tokyo**
Spandrel Panels	Curtain Wall Consultant
Bent heavy gauge aluminum	**Benson Industries**

G
Detail section at horizontal mullion
1 Aluminum horizontal mullion cap
 (customized extrusion)
2 Insulated clear vision glass
3 Customized aluminum panel with custom
 color coating

H
Detail plan of typical vertical mullion
at column
1 Mullion with structural glazing
 (unitized system)
2 Intermediate mullion
3 Customized horizontal extrusion

I
Section of typical office wall
1 Blind pocket
2 Horizontal mullion cap,
 customized extrusion
3 Customized aluminum panel
4 Fresh air intake

J
Section of refreshment zone wall
1 Aluminum sunshades
2 Spandrel glass panel
3 Fresh air intake
4 Customized aluminum panel

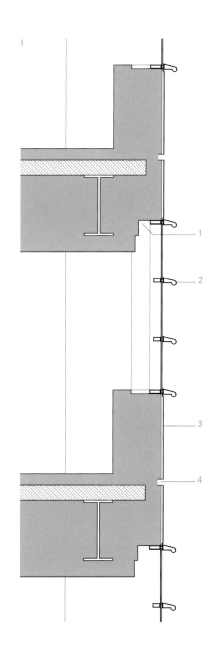

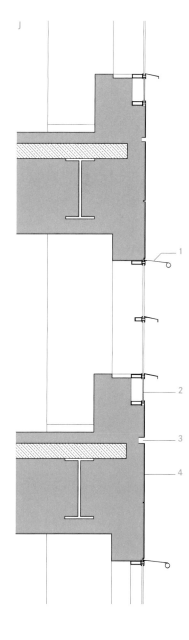

PLAZA TOWER
COSTA MESA

A
West elevation, scale 1:750

B
Site plan

A

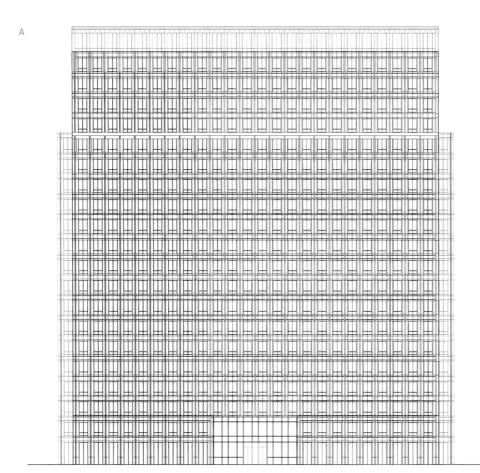

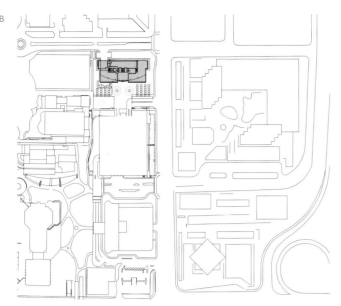

B

Context and Site: Rising 21 stories, Plaza Tower is located in the South Coast Plaza Town Center of Costa Mesa, California. The position of the building relates back to the city, toward which it presents its dramatically curved façade. It was also important that views of Plaza Tower from the nearby highway be accentuated to heighten the building's stature as a business address.

Initial block massing studies envisioned the building as more of a square tower with its main façades facing east-west. CP&A reoriented the building and elongated the façades.

Architectural Form and Expression: Plaza Tower's curved façade relates to its approach by car and establishes a very formal front at its entrance. The formality and nobility of the building are strengthened by the double loggias and setbacks at the 17th and 21st floors. The curved tower grows from a two-story rectangular podium in plan that reaches out to visitors and mediates the building's scale. Two diminutive, slender blocks hug the tower's sides and extend up to the 16th floor.

Curtain Wall Components: The form and materials of Plaza Tower are well integrated. In fact, one might say that the choice of stainless steel prompted the tower's curved wall, as this material sings in the radiance of such a surface. Plaza Tower was designed shortly after 777 Tower in Los Angeles, one of the firm's first forays into stainless steel curtain walls, and CP&A was eager to experiment further with the material, which the architects found more appropriate to the context of L.A. than stone. 777 Tower also has a curved façade, which makes the stainless steel wall gleam under virtually any light, bringing to life the best reflective qualities of this elegant material. Stainless steel is a material that connotes strength, durability, and precision. It is also a material of great visual and sensual richness. The design takes maximum advantage

of these qualities to produce a building wall of sophistication and beauty.

Plaza Tower's ratio of glass to opaque wall (40 percent to 60 percent) is a response to the California Energy Code, and makes the stainless steel the predominant material. The stainless steel is a Type 316, which is particularly resistant to staining. Designed with a double grid of vertical and horizontal ribs, the stainless steel panels with their linen-embossed finish give the exterior wall scale and texture, an esthetic expression of advanced technology.

While Plaza Tower's stainless steel curtain wall is essentially two-dimensional, the use of vertical bullnoses positioned between the windows gives the wall some depth. The rounded edges of these brush-finished ribs catch the light, forming partial or complete traceries of highlights on the wall.

The glass chosen for this curtain wall makes the building appear as a shimmering, highly polished object. The insulated units have a low-e coating on the number 2 surface to mitigate heat gain. The glass also has a moderately reflective stainless steel coating that complements the cladding material.

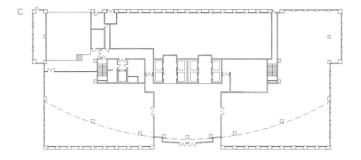

Detail view of curtain wall and third floor
corner setback

East entrance

East elevation

View of north-west elevation

C
Ground floor plan

D
Building base corner

E
Wall elevation and section at upper floor
1 Type 316 stainless steel cladding
2 25.4mm insulated vision glass
3 Type 316 stainless steel mullion cover
4 1.8mm type 316 stainless steel flat
   formed panels
5 Stainless steel accents

D

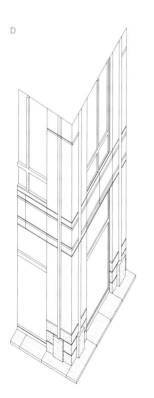

E

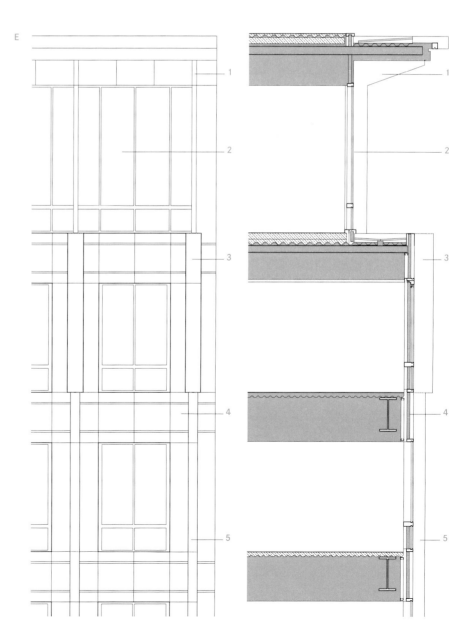

F
Typical floor plan

G
Typical re-entrant corner
1 Type 316 stainless steel window frame
2 Extruded aluminum unitized frame
3 25.4mm insulated vision glass
4 1.8mm type 316 stainless steel flat
   formed panels
5 Type 316 stainless steel vertical mullion

Detail view of third floor corner setback

Curtain wall detail

View of lower level curtain wall
under construction

View of west elevation under construction

Curtain wall visual mock-up

Location
Costa Mesa, California
Dates
1989 – 1991
Client
600 Anton Boulevard Associates, IBM
Building Program
Offices
Height
86.6 meters; 21 floors
Building Structural System
Steel frame
Curtain Wall System
Unitized
Mullions
Stainless steel
Spandrel Panels
Opacified glass at the bottom of each unit
Glass Type
Reflective glass
Lighting
Metal halide uplights under soffits on floors 17, 21

Curtain Wall Manufacturer
Benson Industries
CP&A Project Team
Design Principal: Cesar Pelli
Collaborating Designer and Project Principal:
Fred Clarke
Design Team Leader: Jun Mitsui
Project Managers: Bruce Sielaff, Cherie Santos
Designers: Kevin Burke, Scott Aquilina, Hiroyuki
Kataoka, David Toti
Associate Architect
CRSS Inc.
Structural Engineer
CBM Engineers
Curtain Wall Consultant
Peter M. Muller

F

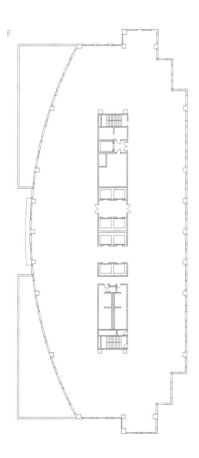

G

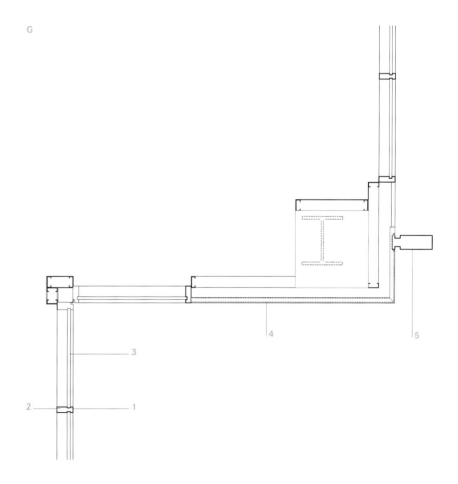

PETRONAS TOWERS
KUALA LUMPUR

A

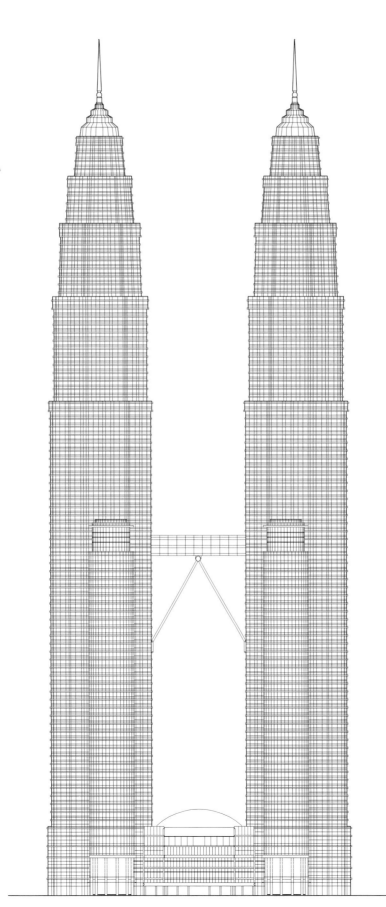

A
Twin tower elevation, scale 1:2000

B
Site plan

B

Context and Site: Malaysia is among the fastest growing countries in the Pacific Basin. To meet the demand of urban growth for Kuala Lumpur, its Federal Capital, the Malaysian Government designated the Selangor Turf Club and its surrounding land, strategically located in the heart of the commercial district Golden Triangle, for the development of a new "city-within-a-city." CP&A won an international architectural competition to design Phase One of the Kuala Lumpur City Centre as part of the master plan for the 100-acre site.

Architectural Form and Expression: The towers express traditional Malaysia, but they also express the new Malaysia: a rapidly industrializing country with a dynamic economy. The character of these towers was of great concern to the organizers of the project, who had a strong desire that the architecture be "Malaysian." The design of the two 88-story towers responds to the climate, to the dominant Islamic culture, and to the sense of form and patterning in traditional Malaysian buildings and artifacts.

The geometry of the towers is based on Islamic geometric traditions. The plan takes the form of two interlocked squares that create an eight-pointed star – perhaps the most important geometric form underlying Islamic designs. To this form are superimposed eight semi-circles in the inner angles of the star creating a 16-branch form. In each of the 16 inner angles there are smaller semi-circular forms expressing the main structural columns of the building. The towers are figurative and symmetrically composed, with a void between the two. The power of the void is made more explicit by the pedestrian bridge that connects the two towers at the 41st and 42nd floors. The bridge with its supporting structure creates a portal to the sky 170 meters high. As it ascends, each tower steps back six times. In the upper setbacks, the walls tilt gently towards the center, completing the form.

Curtain Wall Components: The predominant material in the curtain wall is stainless steel, designed in such a way that the main reading is of bullnoses and sunshades, with the glass subdued. Because this building is in the tropics near the equator, the sun pervades the building on all sides and sunshades that completely surround the towers are a necessity. The projecting bullnoses and sunshades are the primary elements in expressing the 16-branch form of each tower plan. Projecting out from the building on brackets just above the vision glass, the teardrop-shaped sunshades of 32mm stainless steel have a number 4 brushed finish that runs horizontally. During modeling, the angle of the airfoil-shaped elements was adjusted to maximize shading while minimizing staining from water runoff. Just below each line of vision glass are two stainless steel bullnoses with the same brushed finish. The stainless steel spandrel panels and roll-formed column covers are of 16mm-thick material with a linen finish. Fabricators were careful to ensure that the grain of the stainless steel ran horizontally for a consistent appearance. This orientation means that reflections on sunlight are read in parallel to the ribbon windows, emphasizing the towers' banded composition. The 30,000 stainless steel curtain wall panels have a double set of anchors to provide structural redundancy.

The vision glass selected is non-insulated, light green-tinted. The tinting is of just the right wavelength to cancel the sun's infrared heat from entering the building. Laminated glass provides an extra measure of safety and psychological comfort for office workers in two of the world's tallest buildings.

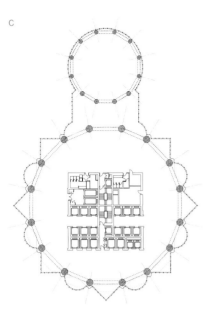

C
Tower plan

D
Ground floor plan

E
Tower section

F
Detail plan tower, half round

G
Detail plan tower, square corner
1 Stainless steel sunscreen tube
2 Prefinished aluminum curtain wall frame
3 Ring beam above
4 Structural column with cladding
5 Stainless steel column enclosure
6 Edge of slab

Towers in city skyline at sunrise

South-west elevation

Detail view of tower base at sunset

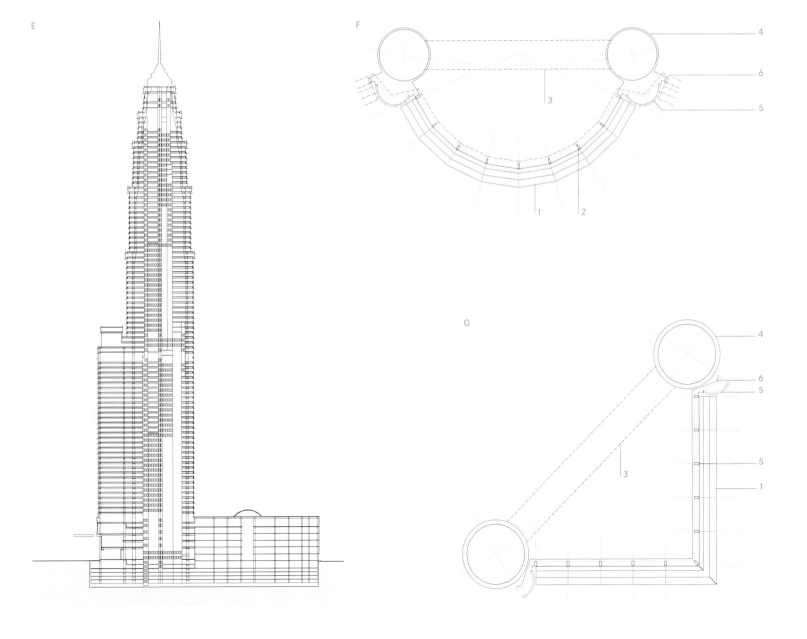

Detail view up tower

Towers under construction

Tower base under construction

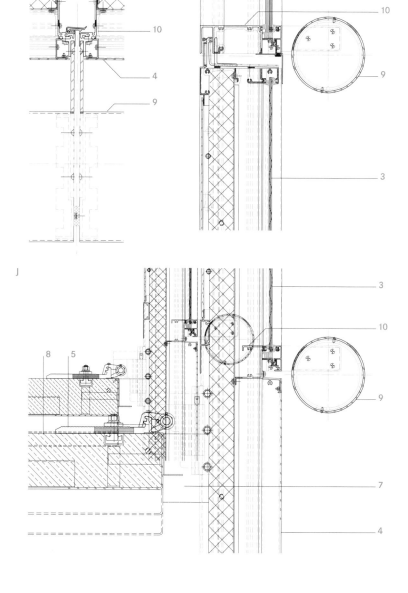

Location
Kuala Lumpur, Malaysia
Dates
1992–1997
Client
Kuala Lumpur City Centre Sendirian Berhad
Building Program
Headquarters
Height
451.9 meters; 88 floors
Building Structural System
Core and cylindrical tube frame system constructed entirely of cast-in-place high-strength concrete (up to Grade 80). Floor framing at tower levels : concrete fill of conventional strength on composite steel floor deck and composite rolled steel framing
Curtain Wall Type
Unitized
Mullions
Stainless steel

Sunshades
Stainless steel
Spandrel Panels
Stainless steel, glass
Glass Type
Vision glass, laminated
CP&A Project Team
Design Principal: Cesar Pelli
Collaborating Designer and Project Principal:
Fred Clarke
Design Team Leader: Jon Pickard
Project Manager: Lawrence Ng
Designers: John Apicella, David Coon, Edward Dionne, Peter Follett, Michael Hilgeman, Russell Holcomb, Alison Horne, Gregg Jones, Vlad Simionescu, Heather Young, David Chen, John Clegg, Jerome del Fierro, Roberto Espejo, Sophie Harvey, Kristin Hawkins, Steven Marchetti, Robert Narracci, Dean Ober, Mark Outman, Enrique Pelli, Neil Prunier, Roger Schickedantz, BJ Siegel, David Strong, Jane Twombly
Associate Architect
Adamson Associates

Structural Engineer
Thornton-Tomasetti Engineers
Ranhill Bersekutu Sdn. Bhd
Curtain Wall Consultant
Israel Berger & Associates

H
Curtain wall plan detail of vertical mullion

I
Curtain wall section detail at sill

J
Curtain wall section detail anchorage
system at floor

K
Typical curtain wall section

L
Curtain wall section detail of sunscreen
 1 Stainless steel sunscreen tube
 2 Pre-finished aluminum bracket
 3 Typical glass spandrel:
     prefinished 3mm aluminum panel, rigid
     insulation, aluminum pan (air/vapor barrier),
     spandrel glass
 4 Metal spandrel
 5 Curtain wall anchorage system
 6 Finished floor
 7 Smokeseal and firestop
 8 Tower structural floor slab
 9 Stainless steel bullnose tube attached to
     curtain wall with prefinished aluminum
     bracket anchored to curtain wall
10 Prefinished aluminum curtain wall frame
11 Prefinished aluminum curtain wall frame
     with integrated blind unit
12 Finish ceiling
13 Vision glass, laminated
14 Ring beam above
15 Structural column with cladding
16 Stainless steel column enclosure
17 Edge of slab

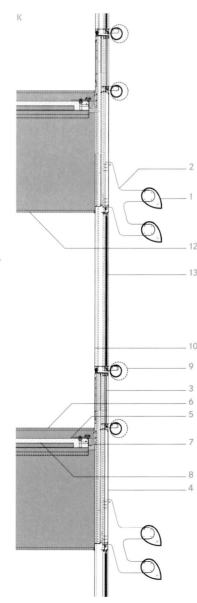

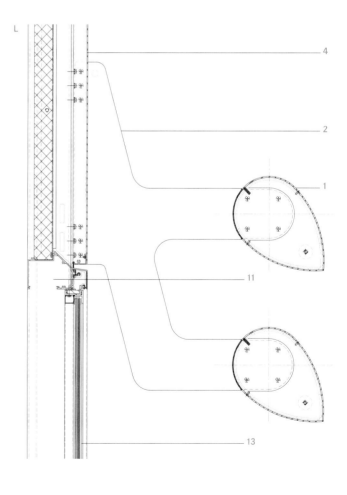

STONE

FOREST RESIDENTIAL TOWER
TOKYO

A

A
East elevation, scale 1:1000

B
Site plan

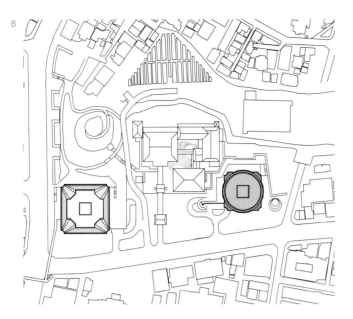

Context and Site: The Forest Residential Tower is part of the Atago Green Hills complex, comprising offices, residences, and shops adjacent to Mt. Atago.

Two 42-story towers – the Mori Office Tower and the Forest Residential Tower – lie side by side. Forest Tower houses luxury residences and is clad with precast panels of integral color ceramic tiles and ribbon windows.

Architectural Form and Expression: Forest Residential Tower is a dramatically sculpted building, starting as a square block at its base. As it rises, the corners are chamfered, and then further splay near the tower top. Each of the four façades is bowed with horizontal bands of balconies for the apartment units. These curved bands further express the tower as a rounded form emerging from a square one, which becomes fully rounded at the top.

Curtain Wall Components: In marked contrast to the nearby glassy Mori Office Tower, the Forest Residential Tower's predominant curtain wall material is Japanese ceramic tile. This material is prevalent in Japanese buildings, as well as in handcrafts – it is a culturally resonant material. The tile curtain wall is composed of integrally colored ceramic tiles measuring approximately 75mm by 150mm, applied to a precast concrete back-up panel 150mm thick. The concrete and tile panels are hoisted into place by crane and anchored to the building's steel structure.

The benefits of this material became apparent after it was determined that a stone curtain wall system would not work with the project budget. In addition to the lower cost and cultural affinity, ceramic tile offers a wider range of color choice, and better control over the colors selected (some types of stone can have wide variations). The chamfered corners of the tower

are rendered in dark brown tile, while the surfaces of the tower's core (primarily the curved balconies) are clad in cream-colored tile. As the chamfers splay open toward the top, and the tower is crowned in a fully rounded form, brown tile predominates. The horizontal expression of the tower is literally underlined by lighter precast concrete bullnoses found at the top and bottom of the ribbon windows. The top bullnoses are larger in diameter, and serve to express the tower's individual floors. The thinner bullnose element at the windows' sill stretches across the balcony as a railing sill.

The curtain wall glass was selected for its transparency, with little or no reflective quality. This allows the scale of the building to be easily read and permits residents unobstructed views of the surrounding city. Mullions holding glass are aluminum, painted in a shade that is complementary to the colors of the tile and concrete bullnose.

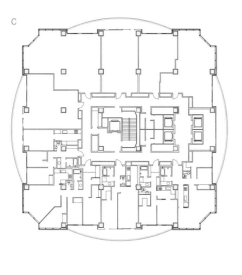

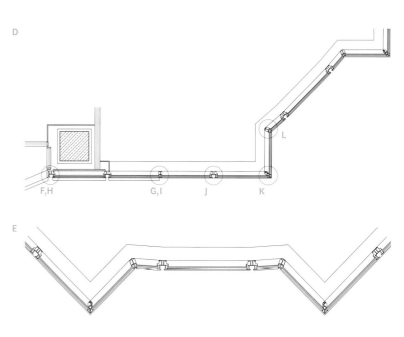

East elevation from street level

North elevation from street level

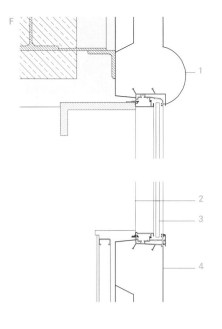

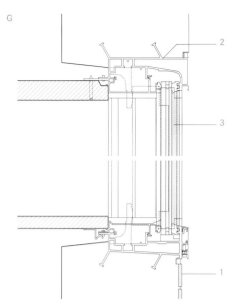

North elevation

South elevation

C
Typical lower floor plan (level 20)

D
Partial façade plan of typical floor

E
Partial façade plan of typical floor at corner

F
Façade section detail, drawing D
1 Precast concrete bullnose
2 Fluoropolymer-coated extruded aluminum
  mullion, cast in concrete
3 Insulated glass with 6mm airspace
4 Precast concrete panel

G
Façade section detail, drawing D
1 Precast concrete panel
2 Fluoropolymer-coated extruded
  aluminum mullion
3 Insulated glass with 6mm airspace

H
Façade plan detail, drawing D
1 Precast concrete panel
2 Fluoropolymer-coated extruded
  aluminum mullion
3 Insulated glass with 6mm airspace
4 Window washing track

I
Façade plan detail, drawing D

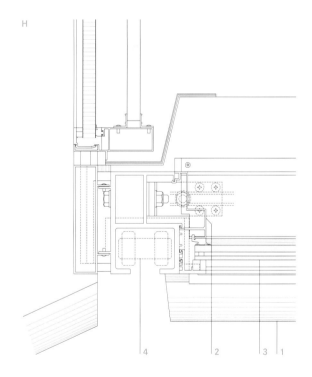

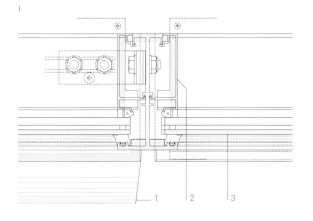

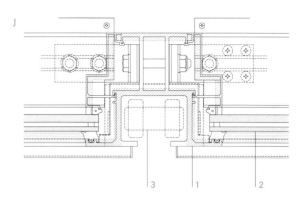

Tower base under construction

South elevation under construction

Detail of tower top

Detail of curtain wall and curved balcony

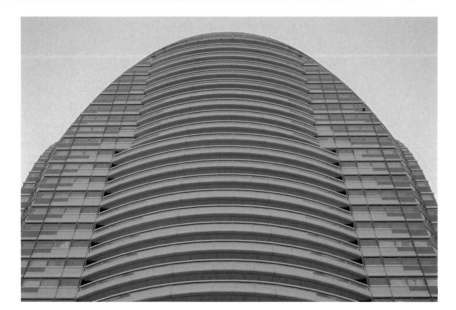

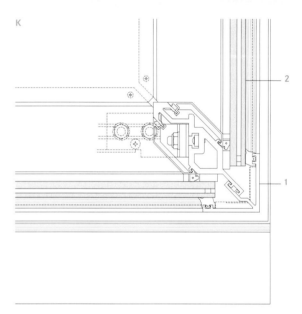

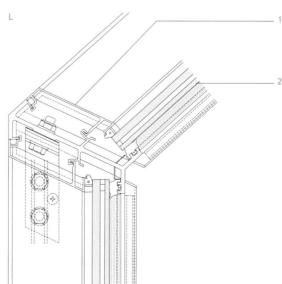

Location
Tokyo, Japan
Dates
1995–2001
Client
Mori Corporation
Building Program
Residential
Height
157.21 meters; 42 floors
Building Structural System
Reinforced concrete with precast concrete beams
Curtain Wall Type
Pre-cast concrete spandrel panels and knock-down aluminum mullions
Mullions
Fluoropolymer-coated aluminum
Spandrel Panels
Precast concrete, tile-embedded finish
Glass Type
Insulated clear glass

Curtain Wall Manufacturer
Takahashi Curtain Wall (precast concrete)
CP&A Project Team
Design Principal: Cesar Pelli
Collaborating Designer and Project Principal: Fred Clarke
Design Team Leader: Gregg Jones
Designers: Takahiro Sato, Pablo Lopez, Natasha Boyd, Projjal Dutta, Keith Krolak, Martina Lind, Marcella Staudenmaier
Associate Architect
Cesar Pelli & Associates Japan Inc., Tokyo, Japan
Structural Engineer
Mori Building Co.
Curtain Wall Consultant
Peter M. Muller / Benson Industries

J
Façade plan detail, drawing D

K
Façade plan detail, drawing D

L
Façade plan detail, drawing D
1 Extruded aluminum mullion
2 Insulated glass
3 Window washing track

M
Typical floor section at corner

N
Tower top section
1 Precast concrete panel with ceramic tile facing
2 Fluoropolymer-coated, extruded aluminum mullion, cast in concrete

M

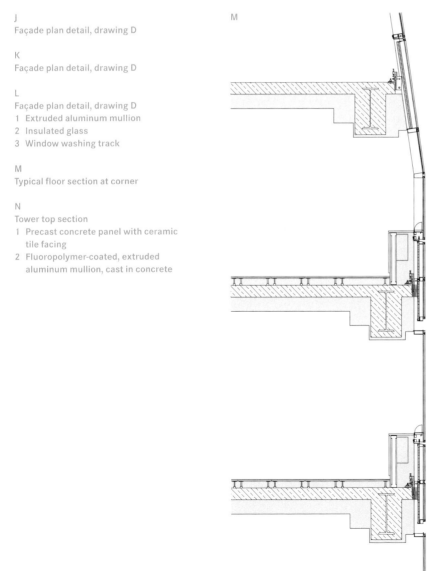

N

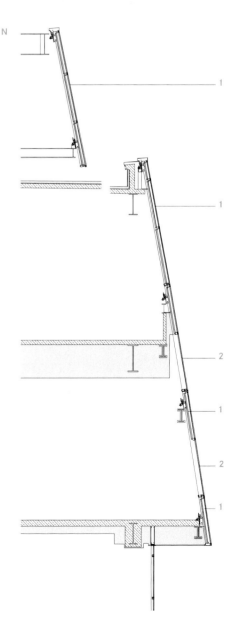

1900 K STREET
WASHINGTON

A
East elevation, scale 1:400

B
Site plan

A

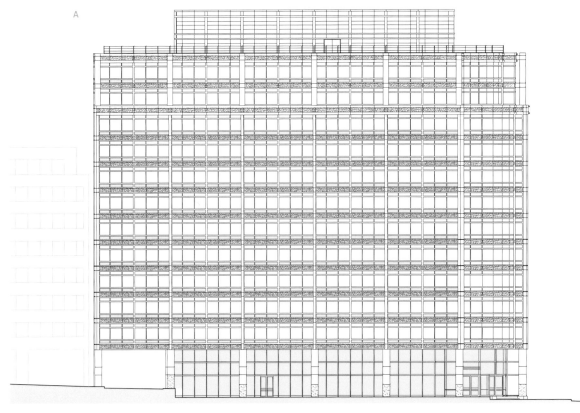

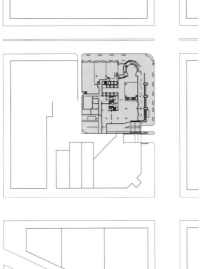

Context and Site: Strategically positioned at the corner of 19th and K Streets in the heart of Washington's central business district, 1900 K Street offers tenants a prestigious and convenient address within the city's Golden Triangle. Low-rise office buildings of controlled height and volume characterize the site. The K Street corridor is one of Washington's greatest concentrations of dismal buildings, so there is very little here to relate to contextually. The building, instead, establishes a new benchmark of quality and design with finely crafted and novel curtain wall materials.

Architectural Form and Expression: The building's height and massing maintains the continuity of the street walls along 19th and K Streets, and conforms to the strict limitation (13 stories) imposed by Washington's zoning laws. The office building contains 2508 square meters on each floor, with retail shops at ground level and parking below.

Below grade there is an English basement for office space, which is connected to the main entrance by a grand stair and light well. Three levels of parking are located below the English basement, accessed by an alley west of the building.

The building's form is essentially an expression of the maximum allowable envelope according to zoning. Recognizing the corner, the building shifts gears from a rectilinear structure to a curved one, and then switches back again — a contemporary interpretation of Louis Sullivan's design for the Carson Pirie Scott store in Chicago, of 1899.

Curtain Wall Components: Because the building could not be inventive in its form (which was strictly regulated) the surface becomes its primary instrument of expression. Stainless steel mullions, column covers, and spandrel panels impart a richness of materials and warm colors rarely seen in this city precinct. A series of round, stainless steel-sheathed columns, marching in front of the penthouse floors, expresses the poured concrete structure and contributes to visually define the two-story-tall cornice set back from the building mass. The columns translate down the curtain wall through paired column covers, to emerge once again at street level in their full, muscular form. The 9-meter structural module is halved on the curtain wall, expressed in the thinner vertical elements. Weaving behind them are delicate horizontal bullnoses that frame the windows and spandrel panels.

The material's richness is accented by the rounded shapes, which give the curtain wall a three-dimensional quality. The number 4 brushed finish on the stainless curved surface runs vertically on horizontal members and vice versa, catching the light and heightening the material's sculptural impact. A subtle transformation occurs at the corner, where the curved stainless steel elements flatten to two dimensions.

Spandrel panels of slate — a novel material for curtain walls — give the building a further sense of refinement and reiterate the horizontal emphasis. Imported from Kirksville, England, the slate is a dark grayish green, with minimal white veining. The pieces are approximately 450 mm high, 1520 mm long, and 30 mm thick, with a natural cleft finish. Curved pieces of slate are used at the corner and have a honed finish (this further communicates the fact that materials on the curved wall are treated differently from those on the street walls).

The glass throughout the building is a clear, insulated material with a low-e coating for energy performance. There is no tinting or reflective coating. Clear 6 mm glass is used in spandrel panels along the street walls, mounted in shadow boxes painted gray to give the illusion of depth. Curved pieces of glass grace the corner, and here the spandrel panels become vision glass extending to the floor. The curved glass elongates reflections, furnishing the building with a visually exaggerated height and a polished appearance.

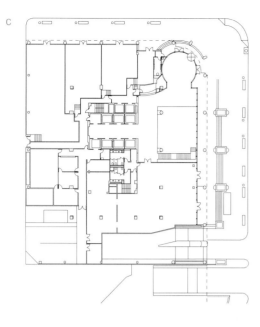

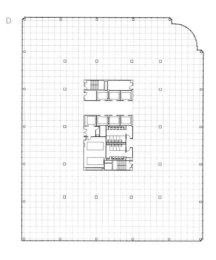

North and east elevations from
19th and K Street

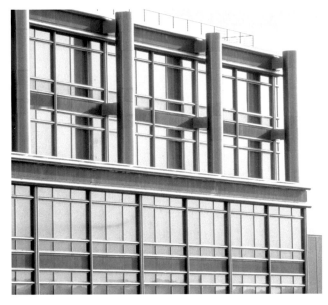

Detail view of curtain wall at penthouse level
and stainless steel-sheathed columns

Detail view of corner setback

C
Ground floor plan

D
Typical office floor plan

E
Plan detail at north-east corner

F
Wall section through setback
1 Bent stainless steel, #4 brush finish, grain
   direction perpendicular to axis
2 30mm green slate panel, honed finished
3 Clear insulated glass, low-e coating
   on #2 surface
4 Stainless steel clad mullion, #4 brush finish
5 Shadow box: 6 mm clear glass, 106 mm
   airspace, painted aluminum
6 Roof construction: precast concrete pavers,
   thermal insulation, waterproof layer

E
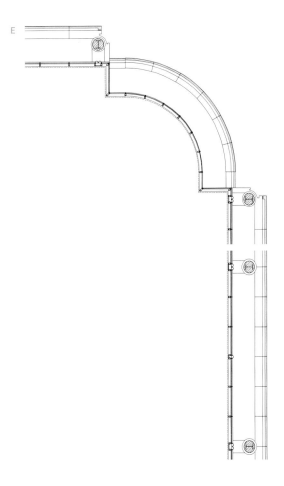

F
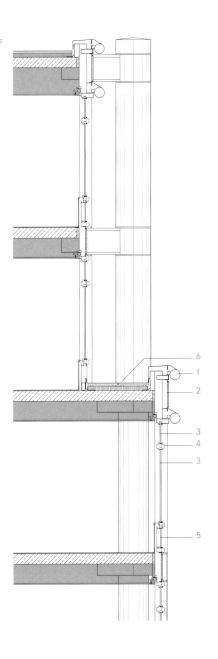

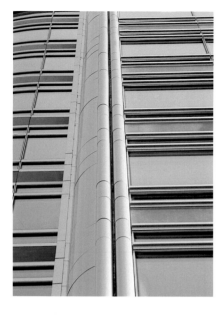

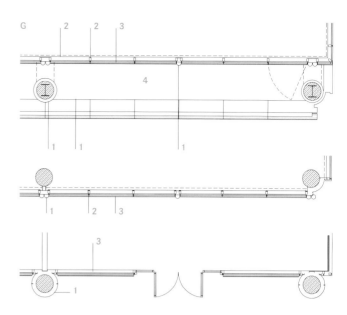

Detail view of stainless steel-sheathed columns

Detail view of curtain wall

Curtain wall performance mock-up

G
Plan details of ground floor (below), typical floor (center), and set back floor (above)
1 Bent stainless steel, #4 brush finish, grain direction perpendicular to axis
2 Painted aluminum mullion, fluoropolymer in custom color
3 Clear insulated glass, low-e coating on #2 surface
4 Pavers

H
Wall section detail

I
Section detail
1 Bent stainless steel, #4 brush finish, grain direction perpendicular to axis
2 Painted aluminum mullion
3 Clear insulated glass, low-e coating on #2 surface
4 Thermal insulation
5 30mm green slate panel, honed finished
6 Painted aluminum, fluoropolymer in custom color
7 6 mm clear glass
8 Steel angle
9 Fire safing

Curtain wall performance mock-up

Location	Curtain Wall Manufacturer
Washington, DC	**Antamex**
Dates	CP&A Project Team
1991 – 1996	**Design Principal: Cesar Pelli**
Client	**Collaborating Designer and Project Principal:**
Kaempfer Partners	**Fred Clarke**
Building Program	**Design Team Leader: Robert Bostwick**
Offices	**Designers: Susana LaPorta Drago, Kevin Burke,**
Height	**Karen Koenig Johnson, Dean Ober**
41 meters to rooftop terrace, 47 meters to	Associate Architect
mechanical penthouse; 13 floors	**Vlastimil Koubek, Architect**
Building Structural System	Structural Engineer
Post-tensed reinforced concrete	**Tadjer-Cohen-Edelson-Associates**
Curtain Wall Type	Curtain Wall Consultant
Unitized	**Raymond Wilson & Associates**
Mullions	
Aluminum clad in stainless steel	
Spandrel Panels	
Stone and shadow boxes	
Glass Type	
Clear glass with low-e coating	
Lighting	
Uplights at exposed columns at setback level	

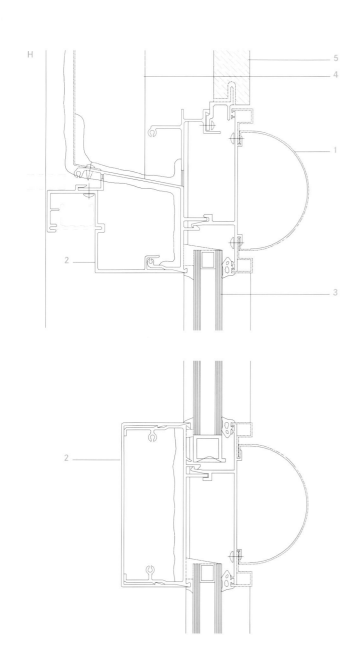

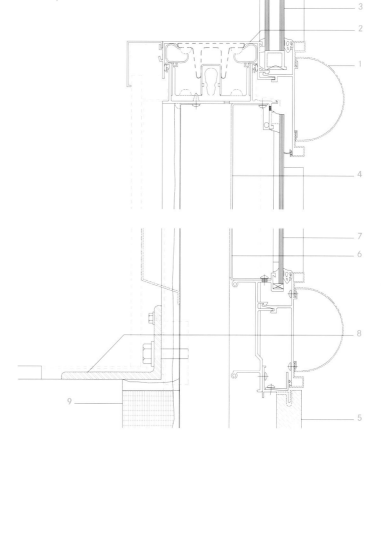

40 **BANK STREET**
LONDON

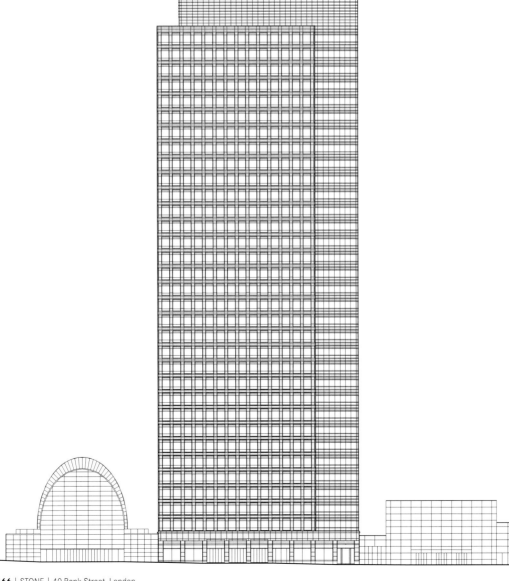

A
North elevation, scale 1:1000

B
Canary wharf site plan

Context and Site: This building is part of a complex of structures that forms the urban façade defining a portion of the southern edge of Jubilee Park – the heart of Canary Wharf's Heron Quay development.

Architectural Form and Expression: The 152-meter building is composed of two interlocking volumes and, with its sister building of 61 meters, provides a warm and inviting civic façade to the park designed by Jacques Wirtz. Between the two buildings, the East Winter Garden acts as the centerpiece to the ensemble.

In sharp contrast to the rectilinear geometry of the surrounding buildings, the glass and steel structure of the East Winter Garden is highly sculptural in character. Its vaulted glass roof, rising 27 meters in height, encloses a grand space that is essentially an urban room functioning as a welcome retreat for workers at the Wharf, or as a setting for informal concerts, performances and other gala events.

The West Winter Garden is an abstract glass structure of cubic volume, located between 40 Bank Street and the Lehman Brothers Headquarters Building, providing a passive retreat and protected pedestrian circulation between Nash Court and the footbridge to South Quay.

Curtain Wall Components: The major volumes of both buildings are clad in warm creamy color Brazilian granite with a flamed finish. The end volumes embraced by the stone blocks of both buildings are clad in metal and glass, responding to the character of neighboring buildings beyond. The metal and glass volumes rise above the stone façades to form a crystalline building top, providing a crowning gesture to both buildings when lit at night.

The proportion of the window openings on the stone curtain wall is designed to exaggerate and enhance the vertical height and scale of 40 Bank Street. The stone panels are treated as ribbons to modulate the stainless steel and glass curtain wall, which is recessed from the stone surface. All window openings in the stone panels are framed vertically and horizontally with a delicate brushed-finished stainless steel. The horizontal mullions echo the shape and finish of the stainless steel. The building's re-entrant corners are clad in stainless steel. The stone panels and stainless steel elements are hung on the curtain wall frame with dry joints between them to allow movement due to temperature differentials between the materials.

The end metal and glass volumes are modulated by a series of horizontal stainless steel tubular projections to enhance the crystalline quality of the transparent glass volumes. Each tubular section is 119mm in diameter and projects 270mm from the glass surfaces, which in turn are held in place by slender mullions. Fine brush finish type 316 is used for all stainless steel elements to ensure a fine, smooth surface less receptive to dirt than other more abrasive finishes.

The glass used throughout the project is a double-pane material with coating on the number 2 surface. This high-performance coating has a shading coefficient of 0.37 to mitigate heat gain, yet it is very transparent.

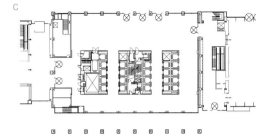

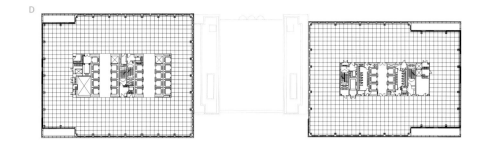

View from Jubilee Park

Detail view of building corner

Detail view of curtain wall

View from Bank Street

C
Ground floor plan

D
Floor plan level 10

E
Partial axonometric at interface between
glass and stone wall
1 Double glazing unit, vision glass area
   Outer lite: 8mm neutral annealed glass,
   16mm airspace
   Inner lite: 4+0.76+4mm clear laminated glass
2 Double glazing unit, spandrel area with frit
   Outer lite: 8mm neutral heat-strengthened
   annealed glass, 16mm airspace
   Inner lite: 8mm heat-strengthened glass
   with custom ceramic frit on #2 surface
3 Double glazing unit, spandrel area
   Outer lite: 8mm super neutral heat-
   strengthened glass, 16mm airspace
   Inner lite: 8mm heat-strengthened glass
4 Granite
5 Stainless steel cladding, superbrush finish
6 Stainless steel round tube profiles,
   dry brush satin finish
7 Aluminum extruded profiles (powder coat)

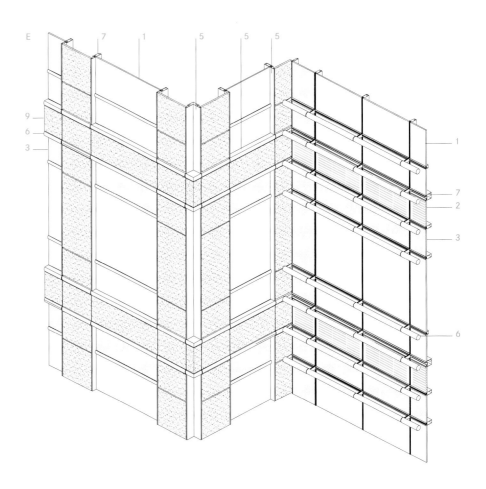

F
Building top elevation

G
Typical section at stone façade
Partial axonometric at interface between
glass and stone wall
1   Double glazing unit, vision glass area
    Outer lite: 8mm neutral annealed glass,
    16mm airspace
    Inner lite: 4+0.76+4mm clear
    laminated glass
2   Double glazing unit, spandrel area with frit
    Outer lite: 8mm neutral heat-strengthened
    annealed glass, 16mm airspace
    Inner lite: 8mm heat-strengthened glass
    with custom ceramic frit on #2 surface
3   Double glazing unit, spandrel area
    Outer lite: 8mm super neutral heat-
    strengthened glass, 16mm airspace
    Inner lite: 8mm heat-strengthened glass
4   Granite

Curtain wall installation

Curtain wall installation

Details of 40 Bank Street curtain wall and
East Winter Garden

F

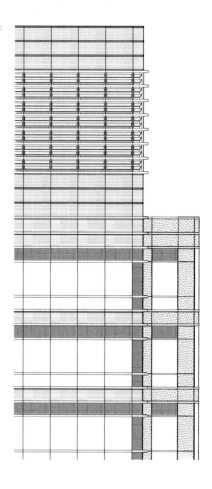

5   Stainless steel cladding, superbrush finish
6   Stainless steel round tube profiles, dry brush
    satin finish
7   Aluminum extruded profiles (powder coat)
8   80mm mineral rock wool
9   2mm aluminum sheet, not exposed
10 Structural slab
11 Structural column
12 8mm stainless steel bracket dry brush
    satin finish

H
Typical section at glass façade

I
Typical plan detail at stone wall

Location
London, England
Dates
2000–2003
Client
Canary Wharf Contractors Limited
Building Program
Offices
Height
152 meters; 31 floors
Building Structural System
Concrete core with steel superstructure
Curtain Wall Type
Unitized
Mullions
Aluminum
Sunshades
Stainless steel, fine brushed finish
Spandrel Panels
Shadow box
Glass Type
**Sealed double glazing unit with high-
performance coating**

Curtain Wall Manufacturer
Permasteelisa
CP&A Project Team
Design Principal: Cesar Pelli
Collaborating Designer and Project Principal:
Fred Clarke
Design Team Leader: Lawrence Ng
Designers: Michael Hilgeman, Marta Damian,
Tomas Delgado
Associate Architect
Adamson Associates
Structural Engineer
Ove Arup & Partners
Curtain Wall Consultant
Adamson Associates

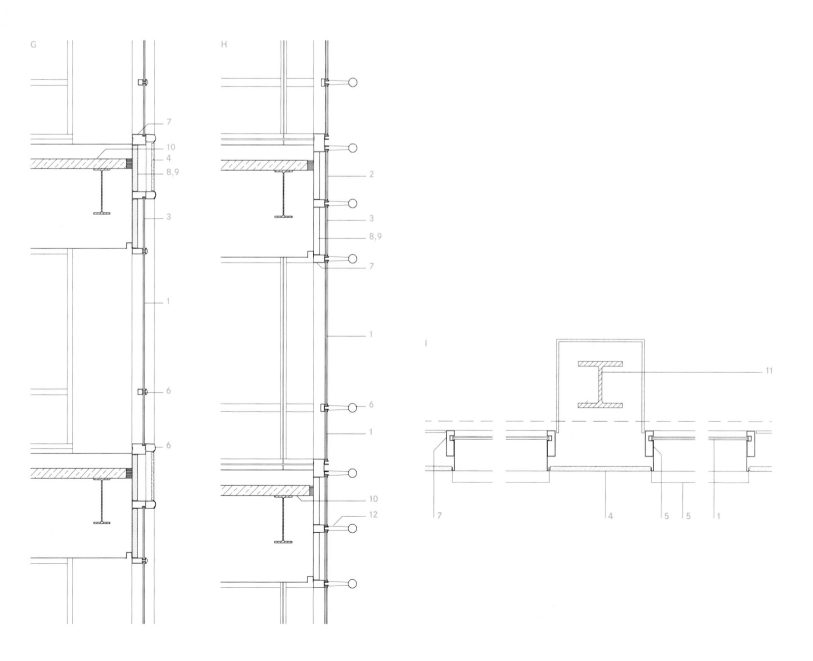

NAKANOSHIMA MITSUI BUILDING
OSAKA

A
East elevation, scale 1:1000

B
Site plan

A

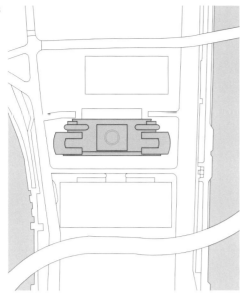

Context and Site: Following an invited design competition, CP&A was selected by Mitsui-Fudosan (one of Japan's largest real estate firms) to design a new high-rise office tower situated on a prominent site on the island of Nakanoshima in central Osaka's Kita Ward.

Situated on a narrow site that connects the Tosabori and Dojima rivers, this 31-story building serves as headquarters to several companies of the Mitsui Group. This part of the island is very dense with development. It is also not much more than a block wide, which means that the building could span from river to river.

Architectural Form and Expression: The narrow site, the island's density, and the opportunity to link the rivers with a building drove the development of a very thin building form, a veritable "book" with its longer sides facing east and west. A sculptural building on this site in this context was not appropriate, so the design focused on ways of expressing the building's slab-like identity. It was determined that the best way to do this would be for each of the building's four sides to respond to the environment.

Curtain Wall Components: The building's façade features elements of the original Mitsui building (demolished in 1999), such as vertical lines incorporating main columns and smaller pillars between them. At the same time, a feeling of openness and sophistication is achieved with a patterned combination of glass, stainless steel, and stone. The design for each of the four façades results in rich, distinct, and unique surfaces that respond to the orientation. For example, the long east façade conveys a sense of substance, depth, and a more traditional solidity at the base of the tower while slowly and subtly transitioning into a more open and glassy expression at the top. This is realized through a steady and subtle reduction in the curtain

wall of the amount of visible matte- and flamed-finished gray granite. The vertical granite piers slide back into the glass wall as the building climbs, while the horizontal stone spandrel panels become progressively shorter in height until they essentially disappear near the building's terminus. Throughout this façade weaves the highly polished stainless steel of the curtain wall, which plays off the muted stone surfaces.

In contrast, the west façade conveys a more uniform and unvarying sense of solidity while expressing the different core elements within the building. Here Brazilian Samba white granite is the predominant material, giving the curtain wall a solid appearance and a canvas upon which the setting sun plays in the late afternoon.

On the curved north and south façades, the curtain wall is rendered as a glass and stainless steel sheath. The south elevation features stainless steel louvered sunshades, 750mm deep, which (in combination with the insulated low-e glass) helps to reduce heat gain into the building. The glass throughout is moderately reflective. At night, the façades' integral lighting system gives the building a distinct image and silhouette in Osaka's nightscape.

C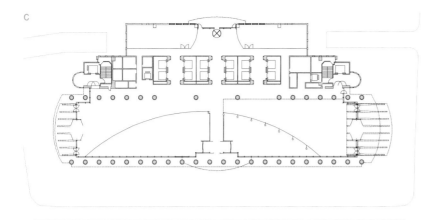

D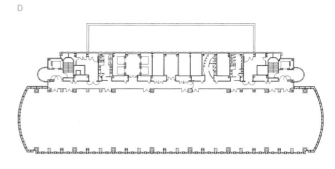

Night view of south and east elevations

East elevation showing spandrel gradation

C
Floor plan – entry lobby

D
Typical office floor plan

E, F
Axonometric detail at lower and upper floors
1 Vertical piers Brazilian Samba white granite, honed finish. Stone piers gradually reduce in protrusion depth as the tower rises
2 Window washing track: custom profiles, stainless steel hairline finish
3 Sunshades: ovaloid sections of stainless steel, hairline finish welded to stainless steel bracket arms
4 Stone spandrel panels: Brazilian Samba white granite, thermal finish. Stone spandrels gradually reduce in height as the tower rises and transform into glass
5 75mm airslot allows fresh air to be introduced, filtered and controlled along the exterior wall at each floor.
6 Spandrel glass: with custom color shadow box
7 Vision glass: insulated units, clear glass with slight reflective coating
8 Vertical accent rod: stainless steel #8 polish finish with special custom cast aluminum fittings at the stack joint to allow for building and thermal movement
9 Horizontal accents: tube and bullnose with stainless hairline finish

Detail view of fireman's refuge area and stair

View of east elevation curtain wall

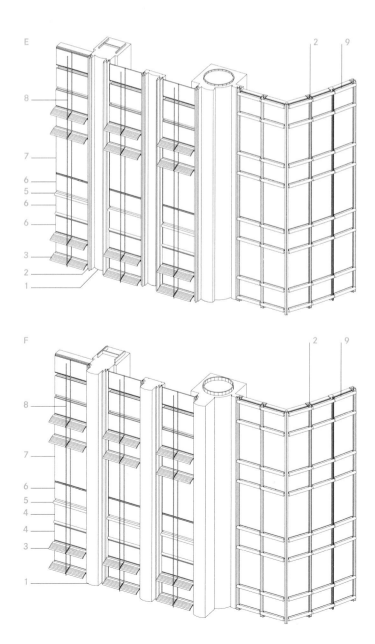

Curtain wall visual and performance mock-up

Curtain wall visual and performance mock-up

Curtain wall visual and performance mock-up

Detail view of south elevation curtain wall

South elevation curtain wall mock-up

G

G
Detail plan east wall
1 Sunshades: stainless steel ovaloid sections
  welded to stainless steel bracket arms
2 Vertical accent rod: stainless steel polish #8
3 Window washing track: custom profile
  stainless steel hairline finish
4 Vertical pier: Custom routered profile,
  Brazilian Samba white granite cladding,
  honed finish

Perforated sunshade corrosion
performance test

Location
Osaka, Japan
Dates
1999–2003
Client
Mitsui-Fudosan
Building Program
Headquarters
Height
140.15 meters; 31 floors
Building Structural System
**Steel construction, partially steel-framed
reinforced concrete and reinforced concrete**
Curtain Wall Type
Metal and precast concrete on the west wall
Mullions
Aluminum with stainless steel cladding
Sunshades
Stainless steel
Spandrel Panels
**Transition from granite to glass as the
building rises**

Glass Type
Reflective insulated glass on east façade.
North, south and west façades: reflective glass
Lighting
Building top is uplit
Curtain Wall Manufacturer
YKK AP, Inc.; Shin Nikkei Company, Ltd.
CP&A Project Team
Design Principal: Cesar Pelli
Collaborating Designer and Project Principal:
Fred Clarke
Design Team Leader: Gregg Jones
Senior Designer: Edward Dionne
Designers: Gabriel Bekerman, Jose Luis Cabello,
Tristan Dieguez, Kay Edge, Pablo Lopez, Robert
Riccardi, Takahiro Sato
Associate Architect
Nikken Sekkei
Structural Engineer
Nikken Sekkei

H
Partial section east wall
1 Entry canopy: stainless steel panel cladding
  with hairline finish
2 Stainless steel panel cladding with hairline
  finish, with conical white granite base and
  thermal finish
3 Stone pier: white granite, honed finish
4 Sunshades: ovaloid sections of stainless
  steel with hairline finish
5 75mm airslot for filtered tenant-
  controlled ventilation
6 Horizontal stack joint: unitized panel
  exterior wall system
7 Rooftop sunshade protection: stainless steel
  panel cladding with hairline finish

I
Typical section east wall
1 Sunshades: ovaloid sections of stainless
  steel, hairline finish welded to stainless steel
  bracket arms
2 Vertical accent rod: stainless steel #8 polish
  finish with custom cast aluminum bracket
  arms at horizontal stack joint to allow for
  building movement
3 Window washing track: custom profiles,
  stainless steel hairline finish
4 Horizontal stack joint: for unitized wall panels
5 75mm airslot for tenant-
  controlled ventilation
6 Spandrel panel: white granite on lower floors,
  gradually diminishing in size, transforming
  into spandrel glass as the tower rises
7 Vision glass: insulated unit, clear glass
  with slight reflective coating

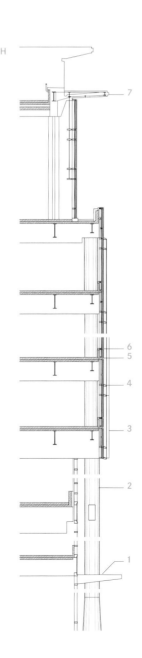

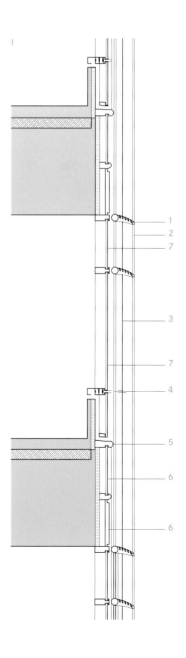

ILLUSTRATION CREDITS